Editor-in-Chief and Founder:
  Lyndon H. LaRouche, Jr.
Editorial Board: *Lyndon H. LaRouche, Jr. , Helga
  Zepp-LaRouche, Paul Gallagher, Tony Papert,
  Gerald Rose, Dennis Small, Jeffrey Steinberg,
  William Wertz*
Co-Editors: *Paul Gallagher, Tony Papert*
Managing Editor: *Nancy Spannaus*
Technology: *Marsha Freeman*
Books: *Katherine Notley*
Graphics: *Alan Yue*
Photos: *Stuart Lewis*
Circulation Manager: *Stanley Ezrol*

INTELLIGENCE DIRECTORS
Counterintelligence: *Jeffrey Steinberg, Michele
  Steinberg*
Economics: *John Hoefle, Marcia Merry Baker,
  Paul Gallagher*
History: *Anton Chaitkin*
Ibero-America: *Dennis Small*
Russia and Eastern Europe: *Rachel Douglas*
United States: *Debra Freeman*

INTERNATIONAL BUREAUS
Bogotá: *Miriam Redondo*
Berlin: *Rainer Apel*
Copenhagen: *Tom Gillesberg*
Houston: *Harley Schlanger*
Lima: *Sara Madueño*
Melbourne: *Robert Barwick*
Mexico City: *Gerardo Castilleja Chávez*
New Delhi: *Ramtanu Maitra*
Paris: *Christine Bierre*
Stockholm: *Ulf Sandmark*
United Nations, N.Y.C.: *Leni Rubinstein*
Washington, D.C.: *William Jones*
Wiesbaden: *Göran Haglund*

ON THE WEB
e-mail: eirns@larouchepub.com
www.larouchepub.com
www.executiveintelligencereview.com
www.larouchepub.com/eiw
Webmaster: *John Sigerson*
Assistant Webmaster: *George Hollis*
Editor, Arabic-language edition: *Hussein Askary*

EIR (ISSN 0273-6314) *is published weekly
(50 issues), by EIR News Service, Inc.,
P.O. Box 17390, Washington, D.C. 20041-0390.
(703) 777-9451*

European Headquarters: E.I.R. GmbH, Postfach
Bahnstrasse 9a, D-65205, Wiesbaden, Germany
Tel: 49-611-73650
Homepage: http://www.eirna.com
e-mail: eirna@eirna.com
Director: Georg Neudecker

Montreal, Canada: 514-461-1557

Denmark: EIR - Danmark, Sankt Knuds Vej 11,
basement left, DK-1903 Frederiksberg, Denmark.
Tel.: +45 35 43 60 40, Fax: +45 35 43 87 57. e-mail:
eirdk@hotmail.com.

Mexico City: EIR, Sor Juana Inés de la Cruz 242-2
Col. Agricultura C.P. 11360
Delegación M. Hidalgo, México D.F.
Tel. (5525) 5318-2301
eirmexico@gmail.com

Canada Post Publication Sales Agreement
#40683579

Postmaster: Send all address changes to *EIR*, P.O.
Box 17390, Washington, D.C. 20041-0390.

Signed articles in *EIR* represent the views of the
authors, and not necessarily those of the Editorial
Board.

Manhattan's Struggle For Human Freedom Against the Slave Power of Virginia

EIR Contents

www.larouchepub.com   Volume 42, Number 19, May 8, 2015

Cover This Week

An 1853 engraving by Alexander Hay Ritchie

"Triumph of Patriotism," George Washington Enters New York City, 25 November 1783

Manhattan's Struggle for Human Freedom Against The Slave Power of Virginia

A Contribution to an Ongoing Discussion

by Robert Ingraham

April 20—There are myths and counter-myths surrounding the early history of the United States of America. It is often difficult for the mere observer to discern what was actually going on, and what the nature of the battle was. This document will demonstrate that from the very beginning, this nation was defined by a titanic war between two opposing forces, opponents who differed not merely on practical political issues, but on the very nature of the human species itself. On the one side was the New York leadership who created the United States Constitution and defined the mission of the United States during the Presidency of George Washington. Against them were arrayed the Virginia combine of the Southern "Slave Power," an anti-human aristocracy who were determined that it would be the slavocracy of the South who would control the future destiny of the nation. This is the story of that battle.

* * *

In the years immediately prior to the American Revolutionary War, four young graduates of King's College (today's Columbia University) in New York City began a friendship, a personal bond, from which sprang forth the leadership of a new nation. This bond was strengthened and deepened during the years of the American War for Independence, a war which also witnessed the beginning of their intimate relationship with George Washington, and later, in 1787, it would be these four,- Alexander Hamilton, John Jay, Gouverneur Morris and Robert Livingston,—who performed the vital role in the creation of the finished form of the United States Constitution, as well as in that document's successful ratification one year later. Beginning in 1789, three of these individuals—Hamilton, Jay and Morris—would form the nucleus of the leadership in the new Presidential Administration of George Washington, a Presidency whose nature can only be grasped by recognizing that it was a "New York Administration."

They were joined and supported by other key New Yorkers, including Steven Van Rensselaer, Philip Schuyler, and Isaac Roosevelt, along with Hamilton's protégé Rufus King, who moved from Massachusetts to New York at Hamilton's urging. Later, the legacy of this grouping would be continued through the efforts of DeWitt Clinton, James Fenimore Cooper, and others.

The protagonists. On the left, Rembrandt Peale's 1800 portrait of Jefferson; on the right, John Trumbull's posthumous portrait of Hamilton.

Even before the inauguration of Washington, stretching back to the Constitutional Convention and earlier, the philosophy and policy of what would become this 1789 New York Administration was ruthlessly and bloodily opposed by the Slave Interests of the South.

There are two related delusions concerning slavery and the American Republic. The first is that the founding fathers were either pro-slavery, or at least tolerant of that institution. The second is that slavery did not emerge as a decisive national crisis until the 1830s or 1840s, or until the Kansas-Nebraska Act of 1854. The truth, is that beginning with the inauguration of George Washington in 1789, war was declared against that Administration by the Slave Power, and beginning with the election of Thomas Jefferson in 1800, the Southern Slave Power unleashed a relentless, unceasing effort to increase its power, expand geographically and ultimately take over the entire nation.

More was at stake than simply the institution of slavery. The first Washington Administration was an experiment as to whether the principles of the new American Constitution, a constitution steered to its completion by New Yorkers, might succeed in practice. It was the Administration of Alexander Hamilton's cre-

ation of a National Bank, and Hamilton's formation of the Society for Establishing Useful Manufactures. The Washington Presidency was the battleground for the creation of a type of Republic never before existent in human history. From the beginning, the mortal enemy of this design was the Slave Power of the South.

Part I
The Beginnings

John Jay and Robert Livingston met as students at King's College in the mid-1760s, and they became the closest of friends until their break in 1792-1794. Within a few years Gouverneur Morris was part of their group, and this trio was to provide the revolutionary leadership for New York State during the ensuing decade. Hamilton, the youngest of the group, was a slightly later addition, but it was this final arrival whose destiny was to be the greatest of them all. All four emerged from, or were linked to a network of prominent New York families, including the Livingstons, Van Rensselaers, Schuylers, and Morrises. Alexander Hamilton and Steven Van Rensselaer both married daughters of Philip Schuyler,

Manhattan's King's College, 1776

and John Jay married one of the daughters of Walter Livingston.

During the Revolution, not only did Hamilton serve as Washington's most trusted aide, but it was Jay, Livingston, and particularly Morris who became Washington's most vigorous defenders in the Continental Congress. Morris and Livingston defended Washington against repeated attempts to remove him from command,[1] and throughout the war, no one fought harder than Morris to secure food, ammunition and medical care for Washington's troops.[2] It is vital to recognize that to a very real extent, the leadership of the later Washington Presidency was forged, so to speak, over the "campfires of war," by individuals who served directly with Washington during that conflict, including Hamilton, Gouverneur Morris (who spent four months with the army at Valley Forge), Henry Knox (later Washington's Secretary of War), John Marshall (also at Valley Forge) and Henry "Light-Horse Harry" Lee. These individuals, together with others not named here, remained unassailable in their loyalty to Washington until the moment of his death.

---

1. For example, the Conway Cabal.

2. In pleading for aid, Morris wrote to John Jay from Valley Forge, "Our troops, what misery! The Skeleton of an army presents itself to our eyes in a naked, starving, condition, out of Health, out of Spirits... without Clothes to wear, Victuals to eat, Wood to burn, or straw to lie on, the wonder is that they stay not that they go. For Heaven's sake, my dear friend, exert yourself strenuously..." Out of the 10,000 soldiers who marched into Valley Forge, 2,500 would die in camp.

In 1774, after the British government closed the Port of Boston, a committee is formed under John Jay's leadership, to organize a new revolutionary government for New York State: the New York Provisional Congress. Morris and Livingston are elected as representatives to the new legislature, and Jay is the first delegate chosen to the new Continental Congress in Philadelphia.

In 1776, the New York Provisional Congress, at the urging of Jay and Morris, authorize their representatives in Philadelphia to vote for independence. Livingston serves on the Committee of Five, together with Ben Franklin, Thomas Jefferson, Roger Sherman, and John Adams, which drafts the final version of the Declaration of Independence. Later that year Jay and Morris author a new constitution for New York State, and elections are held to form a new state government. Jay is elected Chief Justice, Livingston is elected Chancellor, and their ally Philip Schuyler is barely defeated for Governor by George Clinton.

From 1781 to 1783, Gouverneur Morris, together with Robert Morris, are the vital leaders in reorganizing the nation's finances and staving off national bankruptcy, and, together, they found the Bank of North America.

John Jay, from 1779 to 1782, serves as Ambassador to Spain and then, at the request of Benjamin Franklin, proceeds to Paris to aid Franklin (whose efforts are being sabotaged by John Adams) in securing the final peace treaty which ends the war.

Part II
The Constitution

A continuing lie surrounding the United States Constitution is that Alexander Hamilton played a minor role at the Constitutional Convention and had little input into the final document. The truth is that there would have been no Constitution without Hamilton. He was the initiator of the project and, almost single-handedly, responsible for the convening of the Convention in the summer of 1787; and, afterwards, Hamilton was the driving force for ratification in 1788. In addition, he intervened in two crucial and decisive ways at the Convention itself.

Manhattan celebrates ratification of the Constitution, July 23, 1788.

Hamilton's campaign from 1783 to 1787 to replace the Articles of Confederation is well-known, and the details will not be repeated here, except to emphasize his role in initiating the Annapolis Convention, which met on September 12, 1786 and ended two days later with the Hamilton-authored "Annapolis Resolution," calling for the convening of a national convention in Philadelphia in May of 1787, to be attended by all the states.

This was Hamilton's project from the beginning.

The Philadelphia Convention opened with the presentation of the "Virginia Plan," a document which emanated from James Madison. Madison's proposal was a mess, particularly in the extreme weakness of the Presidency and the Judiciary, and the extensive power it granted to the individual state legislatures. More important, the Madison plan had no *intent*; it was merely a social contract. Even worse, the Virginia proposal was followed several days later by the presentation of the "New Jersey Plan," a rewarmed version of the Articles of Confederation. The grim choice between some version of these two bad alternatives would have been inevitable, but, on June 17, 1787, Hamilton met with George Washington and convinced him to turn over the entirety of the next day's agenda to only one speaker, Hamilton himself. On June 18th Hamilton spoke, uninterrupted, for six hours, presenting his own vision for the new government. Historians almost universally deride this intervention, calling Hamilton's proposal the "British Plan" (despite the fact that it bears no resemblance whatsoever to the British government), and claiming that his speech had

no support and little effectiveness. On the contrary! Through his sheer will and the brilliance of his argument, Hamilton transformed the entire nature of the gathering. From the moment of Hamilton's speech, the New Jersey Plan died, and the nationalists gained the ascendency in the Convention. The battle then became one to improve upon the Virginia Plan, to transform it into the basis for a sovereign Republic.

Shortly after his speech, Hamilton left the Convention for most of the rest of the summer. Again, historians point to this as evidence of Hamilton's pique at the supposed lack of support for his proposal, but a major reason that Hamilton absented himself from most of the convention, was due to his status. New York State had sent three delegates, but two of them, allied with George Clinton, withdrew when they discovered that the Convention intended to overthrow the Articles of Confederation. Without them the New York delegation did not have a quorum, and thus lost its vote. Hamilton's official position had been reduced, according to the rules of the Convention, to that of a mere observer. This is why, at the end of the Convention, Washington stated that the Constitution had been signed by "11 states and Col. Hamilton," New York not having a valid vote, and Rhode Island boycotting the Convention.

After Hamilton's departure, it was Gouverneur Morris who led the battle against States' Rights and Slavery at the Convention. More than any other individual, it was Morris who was responsible for the clauses creating a strong Presidency—the American Presidential System—and it was Morris who battled, almost alone, against the institutionalized Slave Power of the South. During the Convention, Gouverneur Morris roomed with Washington at the home of Robert Morris, and it was very clear to all of the delegates that when Gouverneur Morris spoke,- and he spoke more often than any other delegate at the Convention,- the views he propounded were sometimes his own, but often those of Washington as well.

This is what Hamilton and Morris together accomplished:

1) First, the establishment of a strong, independently-elected' Executive, through the Office of the Presidency. Morris was unsuccessful in his attempts to

establish a full democratic popular election of the President,[3] but he and Hamilton were successful in preventing the selection of the President by either the Congress or the State Governments, which were the majority views at the beginning of the convention. They also were able to empower the President with broad executive powers.

2) The inclusion of a broad General Welfare clause, both within the body of the Constitution, and more importantly the Morris-authored Preamble, which charges the National government to protect and defend the General Welfare for future generations.

3). The establishment of a strong independent Judiciary, something which later became a major source of conflict with the Jeffersonians.

4) Morris and Hamilton were the most eloquent champions of nationalism at the convention,—particularly Morris, who spoke repeatedly and passionately as the champion of national unity. He attacked states' rights and localism from every angle and at each time it reared its head.

5) Morris led a critically important fight over slavery at the convention. Practically alone, he waged this fight all the way through to the closing hours of the convention, brilliantly and uncompromisingly. The Three-Fifths clause which vastly inflated the national political power of the slave states was adopted against Morris's intense opposition.

At the conclusion of the Convention, a "Committee of Style and Arrangement" was appointed to write the final draft of the Constitution. The chairman of the committee was Hamilton, and both Gouverneur Morris and Rufus King were members. This Committee did not merely "polish" the final wording of the Constitution. They were given a hodgepodge of individual clauses that had been approved by majority vote, and their instructions were to arrange them into a unified composition. In doing this, nothing that had been already approved was changed, but the wording and phrasing of the final document all derived from the Committee, and, repeatedly, the emphasis in the final

document is such as to strengthen the truly national character of the new government. Among other things, they clarified the General Welfare clause, and they made significant changes to Article III which strengthened the Federal Judiciary.

The great history-changing accomplishment of Hamilton's Committee, however, was its addition of the Preamble to the Constitution. All contemporary witnesses agree that it was Gouverneur Morris who personally authored the Preamble, thus giving the entire document its philosophical intent. Reportedly, some of the delegates, upon receiving the completed Constitution from the Committee on Style, were unhappy with a Preamble they had neither asked for nor authorized, but it remained, unchanged, in the final document. When you read the words,

> *We the People of the United States, in order to form a more perfect Union, establish Justice, insure domestic Tranquility, provide for the common defence, promote the general Welfare,[4] and secure the Blessings of Liberty to ourselves and our Posterity, do ordain and establish this Constitution for the United States of America.*

you are reading not only the words of Gouverneur Morris but the *Principle* which he, together with Hamilton, embedded in the founding document of our nation.

Morris vs. the Slavocracy

The great untold story of the Constitutional Convention is that the slave interests of the South, led by Virginia, were determined and unyielding that the final agreement would lead to a domination of the new nation by the Slavocracy. Their power and their system was to be enshrined, with legal finality, in the founding document of the nation. This included their demands for enhanced political power based on their states' total slave population, for no restrictions to be placed

---

3. Morris opposed the Electoral College, and he was almost alone in demanding the direct popular election of the President. In Morris's view the office of the Presidency embodied a sacred trust between the people and the nation. He wrote, "It is necessary that the Executive Magistrate should be the guardian of the people, even the lower classes, against the Great and wealthy who, in the course of things, will control the legislature."

4. Attempts were made at the Convention to insert specific federal powers in the Constitution, including the power to erect a national bank and the authority to build canals. Morris opposed this because he believed that by enumerating specific powers, the future role of the government would be restricted to those that were specifically named, and that all of these objectives could be achieved through the broad powers embodied in the principle of the General Welfare. After ratification, this was also the view that was adopted by Hamilton.

on the slave trade, for no restrictions on the expansion of slavery into the territories, and for the use of various clauses in the Constitution dealing with property rights to protect slave ownership.

James Madison's original Virginia Plan called for one-to-one representation of the slaves for the purpose of determining an individual state's number of Representatives in the Congress, as well as that state's number of Presidential Electors. For example, in 1790, Virginia had 435,000 free inhabitants and 300,000 slaves, while Pennsylvania had 434,000 free inhabitants and no slaves. Under the Madison Plan, Virginia's representation would be based on 735,000 people.

Gouverneur Morris

They almost got away with it, but there was enough opposition among some of the northern delegates, that on June Eleventh (when Gouverneur Morris was absent from the Convention), James Wilson of Philadelphia proposed the Three-Fifths "compromise," allowing the South to count 60 percent of their slaves towards representation. This would, for example, allot to Virginia representation for 615,000 "people." Wilson's proposal was adopted with eight states voting for it, and two (Delaware and New Jersey) opposed, and that is where matters stood for one month.

On July Eleventh, Gouverneur Morris rose to speak at the Convention to re-open the already-decided issue of the Three-Fifths clause. The record of his speech and the ensuing lengthy debate with James Wilson is not preserved, but it must have been effective, for at day's end, the Convention voted six states to four to eliminate the Three-Fifths clause and to award no representation for slaves. However, the fight was not over, and during the next two days there were heated exchanges, with only Morris repeatedly taking a strong anti-slavery position, in the face of Southern threats to walk out of the convention.

On July Thirteenth, another vote was held, and the Three-Fifths clause was reinstated, with the Southern concession that Three-Fifths of the slaves would be counted for both representation and direct taxation. The vote to reinstate the Three-Fifths clause was six to two, with two abstentions. Morris was the only member of the Pennsylvania delegation[5] to oppose the compromise.

Morris was not yet done. On July 24th he delivered yet another speech demanding that the Convention revisit and remove the Three-Fifths clause. Incredibly, the five-person Committee on the Whole, in response to Morris's intervention, then voted to reinstate full one-to-one representation (!) for slaves.

On August Eighth, when no other delegate was willing to openly defy the ultimata of the Slave Power, Morris rose and faced the entirety of the assembled delegates. He said the following:

> Upon what principle is it that the slaves shall be computed in the representation? Are they men? Then make them citizens and let them vote. Are they property? Why then is no other property included? The houses in [Philadelphia] are worth more than all the wretched slaves that cover the rice swamps of South Carolina... The admission of slaves into the representation when fairly explained comes to this: that the inhabitant of Georgia and South Carolina who goes to the coast of Africa and, in defiance of the most sacred laws of humanity, tears away his fellow creatures from their dearest connections and damns them to the most cruel bondages, shall have more votes in a government instituted for the protection of the rights of mankind, than the citizen of Pennsylvania or New Jersey who views with laudable horror so nefarious a practice. ...
>
> "Domestic slavery is the most prominent feature in the aristocratic countenance of the proposed Constitution. The vassalage of the poor

---

5. Morris resided in Philadelphia from 1781 to 1788.

has ever been the favorite offspring of aristocracy. And what is the proposed compensation to the Northern States for a sacrifice of every principle of right, of every impulse of humanity? They are to bind themselves to march their militias for the defense of the Southern States; for their defense against those very slaves of whom they complain. They must supply vessels and seamen in case of foreign Attack...

On the other side, the Southern States are not to be restrained from importing fresh supplies of wretched Africans... nay they are to be encouraged to it by an assurance of having their votes in the National Government increased in proportion, and are at the same time to have their exports and their slaves exempt from all contributions for the public service..."

Slaves waiting to be sold in Richmond, Virginia. Painted from a sketch made in 1853.

Slavery is a nefarious institution, the curse of heaven on the states where it prevails. Compare the free regions of the Middle States, where a rich and noble cultivation marks the prosperity and the happiness of the people, with the misery and poverty which overspread the barren wastes of Virginia, Maryland and the other States having slaves. Travel through the whole Continent, and you behold the prospect continually varying with the appearance and disappearance of slavery. The moment you leave the Eastern States and enter New York, the effects of the institution become visible,—passing through the Jerseys and entering Pennsylvania, every criterion of superior improvement witnesses the change. Proceed southwardly and every step you take through the great region of slaves presents a desert increasing, with the increasing proportion of these wretched beings.

At the conclusion of his speech, Morris proposed one small editorial change: to insert the word "free" before the word "inhabitants," which would, of course, have eliminated all slave representation. Morris's motion was overwhelmingly rejected, but in the aftermath of the speech, the Convention voted to reinstate the Three-Fifths representation instead of the Committee's one-to-one proposal. This vote effectively ended the debate over slave representation.

The slave trade was debated from August 21st to 28th. South Carolina led the fight in demanding an unrestricted slave trade. Morris counterattacked, speaking repeatedly, even at one point proposing—as a provocation—that the constitution prohibit the slave trade, but that Virginia, Georgia, and South and North Carolina be exempted due to their commitment to "human bondage." This caused a furor on the convention floor. Eventually, James Wilson proposed another compromise, one allowing the slave trade to continue for 20 years and imposing a head tax on imported slaves. Morris spoke sharply against it, but it passed. The effect of this "compromise" was that over the next 20 years, from 1790 to 1810, 203,000 slaves were brought into the United States, compared with only 56,000 in the previous 20 years.

The last slave-related issue was that of run-away slaves. The Convention had already agreed to a clause requiring Governors to surrender criminals for extradition to other states, but on August 28th the South Carolina delegation demanded that fugitive slaves must be included in the definition of criminals. Wilson again proposed a "compromise," whereby slaves would not come under legal extradition agreements, but slave-owners would have the legal right to enter into other states (or hire someone to do this for them), and seize their run-away slaves, i.e., recover their rightful property. This was the origin of all later "fugitive slave" laws. Again, Morris was vehement in his opposition, but it was voted up by the convention.

Ratification

The Philadelphia Convention ended with the proviso that the new Constitution would go into effect only after it had been ratified by nine states. Hamilton initiated the fight for ratification with the publication, on October 27, 1787, of the first of what later would become known as the *Federalist Papers*. Hamilton initially intended his political offensive to be a two-man operation run out of New York City. At the outset he asked Gouverneur Morris to join in authoring a series of essays, but he declined due to prior obligations to Robert Morris in Philadelphia. Hamilton then turned to John Jay, but after Letter Nine, Jay was forced to withdraw because of bad health. Hamilton then chose William Duer, another New Yorker, as his collaborator, but ended up rejecting Duer's submissions as inadequate. It was only then that Hamilton turned to Madison, his fourth choice, to aid in writing the series.

Over the course of 1788, there were several key battleground states in which ratification was in doubt, including New York, Massachusetts and Virginia. In Massachusetts it was Rufus King and Henry Knox who played the key roles in winning over the leery John Hancock and Samuel Adams to ratification, but the fight in New York was the most intense. For well over a month, during the summer of 1788, a ratifying convention was held at Poughkeepsie, New York, and until the final days, ratification was uncertain. The majority of the delegates, under the direction of Gov. George Clinton,[6] were opposed to ratification, but the delegation from Manhattan, which included Alexander Hamilton, John Jay, Robert Livingston, and Isaac Roosevelt, battled ferociously until ratification was secured in late July.[7]

At the end of the summer, the Continental Congress declared the Constitution to be lawfully ratified, and named New York City as the temporary seat of the government.

---

6. George Clinton would go on to serve as Vice-President of the United States under both Thomas Jefferson and James Madison.
7. For more on the New York ratifying convention, see "The Federal Ship Hamilton," at www.schillerinstitute.org

Part III
The New Administration

It was not inevitable that Washington would head the new government. Following his service in the French and Indian War and the American Revolution, Washington had informed many of his associates of his desire to retire from politics. Hamilton and others knew that a Washington Presidency was indispensable to what had to be done next. Neither Hamilton nor any of his close associates were happy with the final Constitution, but as Morris was later to describe the finished document, "it was the best that could be accomplished ... and infinitely better than the existing Articles of Confederation." The task now was to bring the words on the page to life, and to utilize all of the powers granted by the Constitution to secure the permanent continuance of a sovereign republic. To accomplish that, Washington was urgently needed.

Hamilton, Jay, Morris, and Henry Knox all communicated directly with Washington, expressing their belief that the historic mission could not be completed without his leadership. Morris wrote, "Should the idea prevail that you would not accept the Presidency, it would prove fatal to ratification in many Parts ... your cool steady Temper is *indisputably necessary* to give a firm and manly Tone to the new Government ... you therefore must, I say *must* mount the Seat. The Exercise of Authority depends on personal character, and you are the *indispensable* man." Three weeks after authoring that letter Morris traveled to Mount Vernon and spent three days in private discussion with Washington.

Washington was duly elected, and on April 30, 1789, in Manhattan, he was sworn in as the first President of the United States, Robert Livingston, the Chancellor of New York, delivering the Oath of Office.

Washington was the man in charge, and his word was final, at least to his friends and allies, but, from the beginning, it was Hamilton to whom Washington turned for policy leadership. Washington was not a "figurehead," but he recognized in Hamilton that genius necessary for the establishment of the new Nation, and Hamilton's role in the government became so pronounced, so quickly, that Jefferson and his allies began to denounce New York City, the Capital of the Nation, as *Hamiltonopolis*.

The Washington Administration was an experiment as to whether a self-governing Republic—a govern-

Washington's Cabinet. From Washington's left: Trusted New Yorkers Henry Knox and Alexander Hamilton v. Virginians Thomas Jefferson and Edmund Randolph.

ment of, by and for the people—could be created and sustained. Hamilton was the second in command and the recognized leader in matters of policy. John Jay became not only the first Chief Justice of the United States, but he was also the individual whom Washington repeatedly chose for key tasks of great importance, such as the Jay Treaty of 1795. Gouverneur Morris, Hamilton's closest friend, spent the entirety of Washington's eight years as President in Europe, to which he had been deployed in the role of Washington's private agent, his "eyes and ears,"—and during the entirety of this period, it was Morris, rather than the individual U.S. Ambassadors to France, Holland, Britain and Spain, who became Washington's most trusted advisor in matters of foreign policy.[8] There were others as well, who played important roles, including Hamilton's protégé Rufus King and Henry Knox (the first Secretary of War), both of whom moved permanently from Massachusetts to New York; Philip Schuyler (Hamilton's father-in-law), and Steven Van Rensselaer. All New Yorkers. This was the leadership of the Washington Administration in 1789.

_____

8. Morris's intense loyalty and personal friendship with Washington was legendary. In the 1790s, Thomas Paine denounced Gouverneur Morris as "Washington's irremovable representative, both in France and America." In 1799, when Washington died, Martha Washington personally requested that Gouverneur Morris deliver his funeral Oration in New York City.

In 1789 Washington wanted the permanent U.S. Capital to be located in Albany, New York, while Gouverneur Morris lobbied for Newburgh, a city on the Hudson River just north of West Point. Hamilton was adamant that the capital should remain in Manhattan, and it was from Manhattan that the battle to create and consolidate the United States of America as a sovereign nation was directed.

Thomas Jefferson, confronted with this phalanx of New York hegemony within the Washington Administration, and after failing to stop the approval of Hamilton's National Bank in 1791, quit the administration so as to attack it from the outside. The idea that "Jeffersonianism" arose out of a later corruption of the Federalist Party under John Adams, or in opposition to the rise of the Boston Connecticut Essex Junto types, is simply a lie. By as early as 1790, at precisely the time that Hamilton was attempting to create the National Bank and the Society for Useful Manufactures, the Virginia attack on the Administration was at full throttle, and it would reach a crescendo with the signing of the Jay Treaty of 1795.

Hamilton's Principle[9]

In his series of reports and actions between 1789 and 1793 Hamilton did not set forth a "program" nor a "formula" for economic policy. The intent, the *Principle*, underlying Hamilton's initiatives is grounded in the goal of an ever-increasing National productivity, rooted in scientific and technological advancement. For Hamilton, this was the axiomatic principle at the heart of the Republic, without which there could be no republic, and thus the full power of the sovereign National Government, led by the Presidency, must be brought to bear to secure that directionality.

Far too often, Hamilton's financial initiatives are viewed as just that, financial or banking initiatives, and, after Hamilton left office, the functioning of both the First and Second National Banks was frequently relegated to that lower-level status, of a mere financial or monetary institution. To understand what Hamilton was doing, one has to look at the relationship between the National Bank, the Society for Establishing Useful Man-

_____

9. See "The American Principle: Return to the Actual U.S. Constitution," by Lyndon H. LaRouche, <u>EIR</u>, May 9, 2014.

ufactures (SUM), and his *Report on Manufactures*, not as separate initiatives, but one unified thrust.[10]

Hamilton was determined to use the full power of the National Government to drive forward industrial and scientific expansion, and toward that end he battled intensively for a national policy of "bounties" to directly finance industrial enterprises. As Hamilton asked in the *Report on Manufactures*, "In what can it [the national debt] be so useful, as in prompting and improving the efforts of industry?"—and Hamilton proposed that the National Government use two percent of the national debt to finance the creation of a "national manufactory."[11]

Hamilton's *Report on Manufactures*, which was submitted to

Passaic Falls, New Jersey, site of the Society for Establishing Useful Manufactures.

Congress on December 5, 1791, unveiled the formation of the Society for Establishing Useful Manufactures with the words, "It may be announced, that a society is forming with a capital which is expected to be extended to at least a million dollars, on behalf of which measures are already in train for prosecuting on a large scale, the making and printing of cotton goods."

The Paterson, New Jersey works of the SUM were intended as a "pilot project." The 1791 Report to Congress defined an ongoing policy of national manufacturing development through the use of bounties, intimately interwoven with the credit-generating power of the National Bank. In that Report, Hamilton argued that the authorization to undertake such a policy of national development rested entirely in the powers granted to the National Government under the General Welfare provisions of the Constitution.

In January 1792, James Madison, in the House, and Jefferson, inside the Cabinet, declared war. Madison wrote to a colleague, "What do you think of the commentary on the terms general welfare... this broaches a

new constitutional doctrine of vast consequence and demanding the serious attention of the public, I consider it myself as subverting the fundamental and characteristic principle of the Government, as contrary to the true & fair, as well as the received construction, and as bidding defiance to the sense in which the Constitution is known to have been proposed, advocated and adopted. If Congress can do whatever in their discretion can be done by money, and will promote the general welfare, the Government is no longer a limited one possessing enumerated powers, but an indefinite one subject to particular exceptions."

In February 1792, Jefferson circulated a memo, "Notes on the Constitutionality of Bounties to Encourage Manufacturing," wherein he states that import duties were the only legal and allowable means of promoting manufactures, and that direct government support for manufacturing has not been delegated by the Constitution to the General Government, but remains with the state governments.

In late February, during a meeting with Washington, held at Jefferson's request, Jefferson attacked the *Report on Manufactures*, which he charged meant to establish the doctrine that the power given by the Constitution to collect taxes to provide for the general welfare of the United States, permitted Congress to take every thing under their management which they should

---

10. The only thing comparable over the next 100 years was the way in which Lincoln utilized his Greenback policy, in conjunction with the National Banking Acts, as a driver for transforming the nation.

11. Also, at this time the Hamilton-created Bank of New York was used to help finance these nation-building policies, Rufus King was a director of the bank, and Isaac Roosevelt was its president.

deem for the public welfare. According to Jefferson's own notes on the meeting, Washington's response was frigid, and the meeting ended abruptly.

Nevertheless, the Report was never presented before Congress for debate or a vote. One year earlier, the National Bank had been approved by the Senate by only one vote, with Philip Schuyler and Rufus King leading the fight for it, and James Monroe leading the opposition.

Virginia Declares War

The Slave Power assault on Hamilton began from the day that Washington took office. Just as Hamilton, Jay, and Morris were determined to complete the work of the Constitutional Convention, to create "*a More Perfect Union*," the Virginia complex was insanely intent on destroying Hamilton, breaking the grip of the New Yorkers on the new government, seizing power for themselves and spreading both slavery and the Slave Power across the new nation.

The attack on Hamilton began immediately. It was not confined to a policy fight, but included efforts to destroy him politically, financially, and personally. An indication of their intent was the Jefferson/Madison blackmailing of Hamilton to agree to moving the national capital into the very heart of the Slavocracy,[12] in exchange for their cooperation in the national assumption of state debts, an action vital for the establishment

of a sovereign government. The battle erupted publicly with Jefferson's 1791 declaration of war against the proposed National Bank. Then came the all-out the attempt to destroy Hamilton personally through the Reynolds Affair,[13] in which James Monroe played a particularly despicable role.

Jefferson, Madison, and Monroe were on the attack from Day One, at first within the Administration and Congress, but by no later than early 1791, they began organizing a national party. The method chosen was to create Jacobin Clubs, which on the surface were associations sympathetic with the French Revolution,[14] but in reality were tentacles of the Virginia slavocracy reaching into the North. These political clubs became

---

12. At that time Virginia had, by far, the largest number of slaves and Maryland was second in number of slaves.

13. For the Reynolds story, see *Hamilton's Singular Genius vs. Wall Street's Rage*, by David Shavin, available at http://schillerinstitute.org/educ/hist/eiw_this_week/2015/0111/a.html

14. This is not the place to go into a lengthy discussion of the French Revolution. I recommend the *Diaries of Gouverneur Morris*, the only foreign diplomat to reside in Paris through the entirety of that revolution, from prior to the Tennis Court Oath to after the downfall of Robespierre. Morris was of the view that the French Revolution could not possibly succeed due to the non-existence of a republican citizenry in France, and he saw Lafayette, whom he had known since Valley Forge, as a hopelessly deluded romantic, out of his depth, and listening to the wrong people, namely Jefferson and Tom Paine. From the beginning, with the creation of the National Assembly, Morris predicted that the Revolution would quickly pass over into chaos and massive bloodshed, followed by a dictatorship. Whether one agrees or disagrees with all of Morris's views, his prognostications proved precisely accurate. It should be noted that despite their sharp disagreements, it was Morris who saved Lafayette's wife, Adrienne, from the guillotine.

N.Y. Sen. Robert Kennedy In Mississippi

Biographer Evan Thomas wrote of a trip Robert Kennedy took to rural Mississippi in 1967, to hold hearings on housing. He went out into the fields, where he was deeply moved by the scenes of abject squalor and poverty. Later, when he flew home to New York accompanied by his aides, one of them said, "He grabbed me. He said, 'You don't know what I saw! I have done nothing in my life! Everything I have done is worthless!'"

That very evening, he called together his nine children, ages two to fifteen, and demanded that they dedicate their lives to better the world. He told them that he had gone into one windowless shack, where "he sat down on a dirty floor, and held a child who was covered with open sores. He rubbed the child's stomach, which was distended by starvation. He caressed and murmured and tickled, but got no response. The child was in a daze.

"In Mississippi," he said, "a whole family lives in a shack the size of this room. The children are covered with sores, and their tummies stick out because they have no food. Do you know how lucky you are? Do you know how lucky you are? Do something for your country!"

—*Donald Phau*

the vehicle through which the entire New York leadership of the Washington Administration was accused of being "aristocrats," pro-British, and conspiring to establish a monarchy.[15]

To my knowledge, the only prominent Federalist Party leader who ever publicly advocated a monarchy was John Adams. Hamilton, Morris, and Jay were all impassioned in their commitment to republican government. Additionally, actions speak louder than words, and the policy initiatives which Hamilton battled for—and which Jefferson and Madison opposed—would have led to a dramatic increase in scientific and industrial progress, and the concurrent uplifting of the cognitive skills and productivity of the American people,—the true basis for a republic. Most incredibly, the charges of "monarchist" and "aristocrat" which were hurled against Hamilton, all originated among Southern slave-owners, who themselves parodied the lifestyle of the landed English gentry, and amused themselves by abusing their slaves, or in Jefferson's case breeding with them.

The Virginians began picking off and recruiting weaker members from among Washington's supporters. John Jay's intimate friend Robert Livingston went over to Jefferson in 1792, largely because Hamilton had blocked two of his personal initiatives in New York, the first being Livingston's incompetent attempt to create a Land Bank, and the second when Hamilton secured a New York Senate seat, which Livingston coveted, for Philip Schuyler. Tench Coxe is another example, a man who throughout his career—as his private letters attest—was primarily driven by personal ambition. Supposedly Hamilton's trusted assistant, by 1791 Coxe was de-facto Jefferson's spy within the U.S. Treasury, reporting regularly to Jefferson and Madison on everything Hamilton was saying and doing.

This brings up a touchy subject. The story goes that Philadelphia became the birthplace for a new type of republicanism, Hamiltonian in policy but Jeffersonian in spirit. But there are also uncomfortable truths. Philadelphia was the northern stronghold of the Jeffersonian Jacobin Clubs, which later morphed into the official electoral machine of the Jeffersonian Party. From 1791

to 1794, thousands of Philadelphians marched around waving the Tri-Color flag, singing the Marseillaise, donning the Phrygian cap of the sans culotte and addressing each other as Citizen,—all of them pawns of the Virginia Slave Power. Remember, this was during Washington's **FIRST** term as President, *when Hamilton was fighting for the National Bank and the Society for Establishing Useful Manufactures,* and these Jefferson "republican" clubs were deployed to stop Hamilton dead in his tracks. Painfully, it must also be stated that it was not just Tench Coxe. Rather, Mathew Carey, Alexander Dallas, and other later boosters of the Monroe Presidency *all went over to Jefferson at this time,—not later, but in the very heat of the battle between Hamilton and Jefferson.* In a letter dated September 13, 1792, Elisha Boudinot (one of the directors of the SUM), wrote to Hamilton noting that a petition campaign was beginning against the SUM, and that in Philadelphia, "a strong party is forming in that city against the Secretary of the Treasury."

Then, in 1792 Washington appointed Gouverneur Morris as Ambassador to France, and the Slave Power went wild. The slave-owner James Monroe denounced Morris as an avowed monarchist, unfit to represent the United States. Various Jeffersonian allies attacked Morris's "immoral" character,[16] in which they were joined by John Adams.[17] After a lengthy, intense fight, the Senate, despite Monroe's efforts, confirmed the Morris's appointment by a narrow majority.

The Jay Treaty

In 1794, as relations were worsening with Great Britain, Washington sent John Jay as a special emissary to London for the purpose of negotiating a new treaty, intended to resolve many of the conflicts left over from the earlier 1783 Treaty of Paris. (Three years earlier, Washington had deployed Morris from Paris to London to "feel out" the British leaders on the possibility of a new treaty.) The result was what today is known as the Jay Treaty of 1795, and it was the mas-

---

15. This tactic would be used by the Slave Power against its enemies over and over again for the next 30 years right through the 1828 campaign of Andrew Jackson against John Quincy Adams. Abraham Lincoln was attacked in almost the same exact language by Jefferson Davis and his cohorts in 1861.

16. A bachelor until late in life, Morris had a reputation throughout his life as a "ladies' man," which the Jeffersonians as well as some prudish New England Federalists used against him, in much the same way that Benjamin Franklin had been condemned for his attraction to the fair sex.

17. John Adams burned with envy of Washington, hated Hamilton and despised Morris. However, no one seemed to like him very much, either, except his wife, his son, and Thomas Jefferson in his old age.

sive nationwide Slave Power attack on this Treaty which gave birth to the organized Jeffersonian Party.

As in the appointment of Gouverneur Morris to France, the appointment of Jay as a special Ambassador to Britain was strongly opposed in the Senate by James Monroe, and only approved by an eighteen-to-eight vote.

Earlier, after his paramount role in securing ratification of the Constitution by New York State, Jay had been named Chief Justice of the Supreme Court by Washington. In 1792 he ran for Governor of New York against Jefferson ally George Clinton, only to be robbed of the election,

John Jay, by Gilbert Stuart

when the Clinton-controlled legislature nullified the votes of two entire counties that would have given Jay victory. During that campaign, the Clinton forces circulated articles and broadsheets charging that if Jay were elected he would free all of New York's slaves.

Jay spent one year in London, and in 1795 the treaty which he had successfully negotiated was submitted to the U.S. Congress. For more than 200 years that treaty has been vilified by pro-Jefferson historians as pro-British. I will not attempt a "defense" of that treaty here, for there is nothing to defend. Between 1794 and 1814 three treaties were signed with the British: the Jay Treaty, the Monroe-Pinckney Treaty of 1806 (under Jefferson), and the Treaty of Ghent (under Madison), negotiated by Henry Clay and John Quincy Adams, which ended the War of 1812. Unlike the Jay Treaty, the later Monroe-Pinckney treaty was strictly a commercial treaty, and its provisions— negotiated by an individual who had declared the Jay Treaty treasonous—are almost a carbon copy of the Jay Treaty,—a little stronger on a few points, a little weaker on others, but practically identical. The later Treaty of Ghent was a fiasco, with the United States agreeing to the pre-war *status quo*, and surrendering every single one of its pre-war aims. The Jay Treaty, on the other hand, not only secured peace and U.S. neutrality; it also achieved significant commercial concessions from the British, and was successful in resolving a number of critical

issues left over from 1783, including an agreement by the British to surrender all of the forts they continued to occupy on U.S. soil in the Great Lakes region, which, in fact, they did by 1796.

Hamilton strongly backed the Treaty and campaigned for it; Morris believed that Jay could have pressed the British much harder on trade concessions, but that, nevertheless, the Treaty represented a solid success. Once Congress ratified the Treaty, Washington signed it immediately.

The Slave Power declared war. The "Pennsylvania Democratic Society" was organized in Philadelphia, and an invitation sent out for the formation of affiliated societies throughout the Union. In Savannah, New York, Charleston, and many other locations, groups were organized, all professing the same object, to rescue the people from the oppression of their monarchical pro-British rulers[18]

The immediate goal of these Jeffersonian-directed societies was to overturn Washington's 1793 Proclamation of Neutrality and to bring the United States into the European war, allied with the mass-murderer Robespierre (and afterwards with the Directory). The New York society proclaimed:

> We take pleasure in avowing that we are lovers of the French nation; that we esteem their cause as our own. We most firmly believe that he who is an enemy to the French revolution cannot be a firm republican; and, therefore … ought not to be intrusted with the guidance of any part of the machine of government.

The Pennsylvania society resolved that the President had no right to issue the proclamation of neutrality, and asked

---

18. It was in the fight around the Jay Treaty that the Jeffersonians began to attack Washington by name.

"Is our President, like the grand sultan of Constantinople, shut up in his apartment, and unacquainted with all talents or capacities but those of the *seraskier* or *mufti* that happens to be about him?"

Hamilton took the point in rallying the population behind the treaty, but, at an open air mass meeting in Manhattan, Jeffersonian agents attacked the speaker's platform, and Hamilton was struck in the face with a large stone, barely escaping serious injury or death. In Philadelphia, on the 4th of July, a mob assembled and paraded in the streets with an effigy of John Jay bearing a pair of scales, one labeled "American Liberty and Independence," and the other, "British Gold," while from the mouth of Jay proceeded the words, "Come up to my price, and I will sell you my Country." The effigy was afterward publicly burned in the center of the city.[19] A riot occurred in front of Washington's residence in Philadelphia,[20] with death threats hurled against the President.

Dozens of articles were published attacking Jay, Washington, and the Treaty. In New York, Hamilton's enemy and Jay's former friend Robert Livingston took the lead. He authored 16 essays under the name of Cato, excoriating the treaty as a surrender to Britain. In Philadelphia, Alexander Dallas wrote "Features of Mr. Jay's Treaty," which was published by Mathew Carey, wherein he joined the ranks of those calling for a military alliance with our "sister republic" France. Several of the other Philadelphia publishers, including Bache and Freneau, were far more rabid in their attacks on Jay, Hamilton, and Washington.

But the real intent spewed forth from the heart of the Slavocracy. A Jefferson-allied newspaper in Virginia wrote:

Print Collector/HIP/The Image Works

Jacobin mobs in action. "When he returned home after signing the unpopular Jay's Treaty in 1794, Jay ruefully joked that he could travel across the country by the light of burning effigies of himself."

Notice is hereby given, that in case the treaty entered into by that d—ned arch-traitor John Jay with the British tyrant, should be ratified, a petition will be presented to the next General Assembly of Virginia at their next session, praying that the said State may secede from the Union, and be under the government of one hundred thousand free and independent Virginians." And in South Carolina, the Democratic-Republican Society issued a manifesto, declaring, "Resolved, That we pledge ourselves to our brethren of the republican societies throughout the Union, as far as the ability and individual influence of a numerous society can be made to extend, that we will promote every constitutional mode to bring John Jay to trial and to justice. He shall not escape, if guilty, that punishment which will at once wipe off the temporary stain laid upon us, and be a warning to Traitors hereafter how they sport with the interests and feelings of their fellow-citizens. He was instructed, or he was not: if he was, we will drop the curtain; if not, and he acted of and from himself, we shall lament the want of a Guillotine.

South Carolina's Charles Pinckney, who had publicly battled Gouverneur Morris over slavery at the Constitutional Convention and authored the "fugitive slave" clauses in the Constitution, joined in the public attacks on the Treaty as treasonous.[21]

Jefferson vilified the Treaty, and in the Congress James Monroe fought almost insanely for its rejection.

Hamilton fought back. In New York City, under the name of Camillus, Hamilton published, from July 1795 to January 1796, 38 essays simply titled "The Defense," the first one appearing only four days after the attack

---

19. It was during this period that Hamilton publicly referred to the "political putrification" of Pennsylvania.
20. The Capital had been moved, temporarily, from New York to Philadelphia in 1790.

21. Pinckney would go on to support the administrations of Jefferson, Madison and Monroe, and in 1820 provide strong backing in the Congress for Henry Clay's pro-slavery Missouri Compromise.

that was intended to injure or kill him. These essays had such an impact that Jefferson wrote to Madison, urging him to respond: "Hamilton is really a *colossus* to the anti-republican party. Without numbers he is a host within himself... In truth, when he comes forward, there is nobody but yourself who can meet him." Madison sent a letter to Jefferson declining the challenge to confront Hamilton head-on.

Again, even if it is repetitious, it must be re-stated—so that there is no possibility of denying the consequences—that the political war launched by the Virginia Slavocracy was aimed, not at the Federalist Party, but at Hamilton, Jay, Morris, and the New York leadership. It did not begin later, after the "corruption" of the Federalist Party, but from the moment Washington was sworn in as President. And the intent was to destroy Hamilton, ruin his policy initiatives, drive the New Yorkers out of the Administration, and leave Washington isolated in the fight against the interests of the Slave Power.

As for John Jay, he would later be elected Governor of New York State twice, both times with Steven Van Rensselaer as his Lieutenant Governor, and during his second term, he would successfully steer through the legislature and sign into law a bill leading to the abolition of slavery in New York.

Library of Congress

Thomas Jefferson's slave Lucy, sold at auction after his death.

Part IV
The Slave Power

A word of warning—or advice—is required here. It is not possible to grasp the dynamic of the battle between the young nation's New York leadership and the Virginia-centered Slave Power, without an honest, perhaps wrenching, re-evaluation of certain accepted truisms concerning the patriotic tradition in American history. That said, the rest speaks for itself.

It is the case that at the time of the Constitutional Convention, many leading Americans expected slavery to be abolished within a relatively short period of time. Unlike in 1860, when Southern leaders would regularly invoke God to defend the morality of slavery, in 1788 even many in the South admitted to the horror of the institution, and it was apparent to the majority of Americans that the continuation of slavery and the principles of the Declaration of Independence were incompatible. Prior to 1770, slavery was legal in all 13 colonies; but by 1790 all of the states north of Maryland had either emancipated their slaves or taken steps in that direction, and this momentum was spreading to the South. During the Revolutionary War, Hamilton's close friend John Laurens had introduced a bill into the South Carolina legislature for statewide emancipation (for which he received a congratulatory letter from George Washington), and in the 1780s Delaware came within a hair's-breadth of abolishing slavery.

At the same time, between 1776 and 1789 a substantial number of Southern slave-owners freed their slaves, either outright or in their wills. George Washington was one of these.[22] The eccentric John Randolph of Virginia was another. John Dickinson, once Delaware's largest slaveholder, sided openly with Gouverneur Morris against slavery at the Philadelphia Convention and freed all of his slaves by 1787. The most compelling case is that of Edward Coles, one of the largest slave-owners in Virginia, a neighbor of Jefferson, and an individual of equal social rank to that future President. Coles gathered up all of his slaves, transported them to the Northwest Territory, loaded them all out on rafts and barges in the middle of the

---

22. All of the New York leadership were fiercely opposed to the Slave Power. Morris had authored th first proposal for abolition of slavery in New York State in 1778, and in 1785 Hamilton, Jay, Morris, and Van Rensselaer were all founding members of the New York Manumission Society, with Jay as the first president.

Ohio River, climbed up on a crate, and announced to all of them that he was setting them free. He established a fund to aid them in getting started. Upon his return to Virginia, he wrote to Jefferson urging him to do the same thing. Jefferson replied that it was not the right time.

Additionally, in the North, it was believed—or at least hoped—by many anti-slavery advocates that the success of Hamilton's economic policies and the increasing commercial and industrial prosperity of the nation, would lead to the general recognition of the counter-productive nature of slave labor as an economic system and compel the South to abandon it.

What halted this momentum, this directionality, was not the invention of the Cotton Gin, as some historians claim. *It was the election of Jefferson to the Presidency in 1800, and the iron-clad grip over the national government by the Virginia Slave Power for the next 24 years, that changed the future of the nation.* By 1824 the Slavocracy had placed itself in a position of dominant national power, and, except for the fours years of the John Quincy Adams Presidency, it would retain that power until 1861.

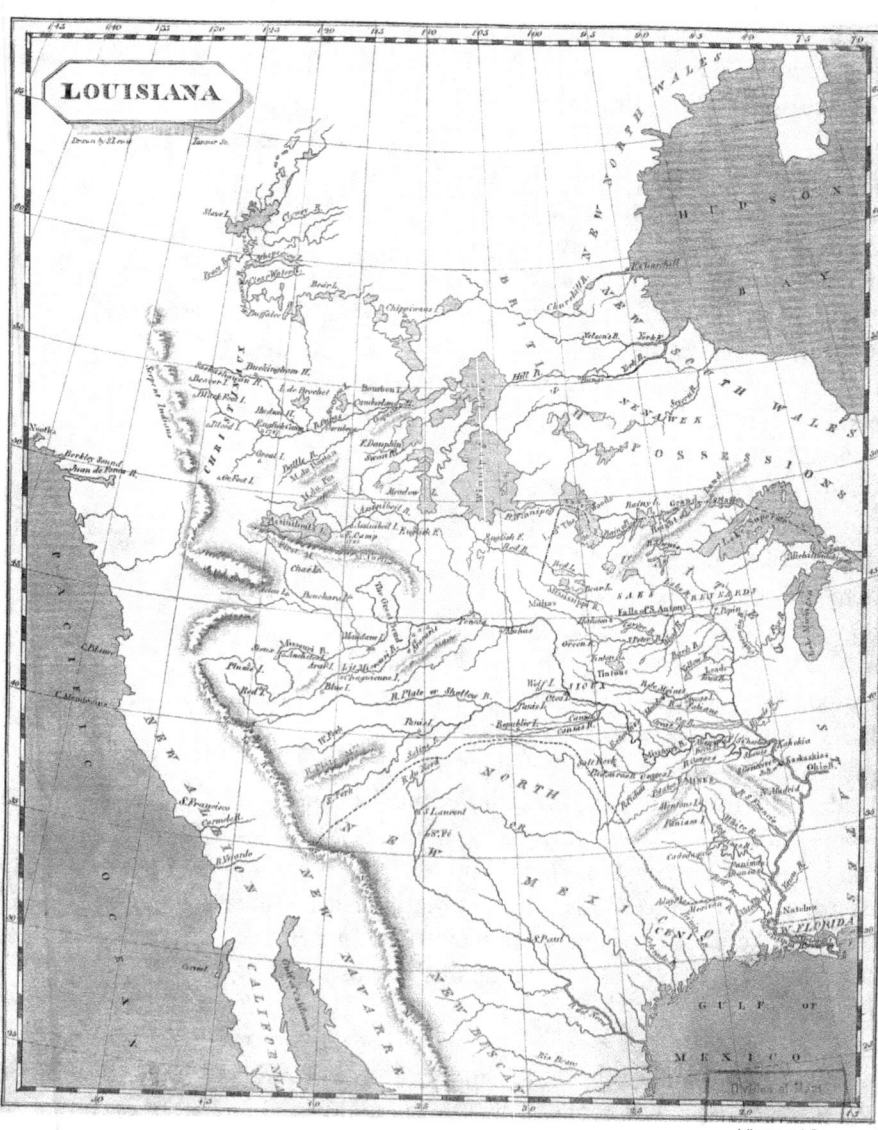

1804 map of Louisiana

Southern 'Defusion'

Between 1800 and 1860, the number of slaves in the United States grew from 800,000 to 4 million.

More important than the simple numbers, was the unyielding Southern determination to spread slavery geographically. During his Presidency, Thomas Jefferson became a vocal advocate for the Southern doctrine of "defusion." Jefferson wrote that spreading slavery into new areas, would benefit the economies of these newly settled regions, while at the same time decreasing the concentration of slaves in the South, making them more valuable as property, and resulting in better treatment for the Southern slaves, thus lessening (defusing) the likelihood of slave revolts.[23]

The 1787 Northwest Ordinance had banned slavery in all of the western territory north of the Ohio River. The South's interpretation of that Ordinance was two-fold: first, that they would simply ignore it, continue to bring slaves into the Northwest, and eventually overturn the ban on slavery, and second, that since no mention was made of the area south of the Ohio River, that this area was de-facto open for slavery. Two new states,

---

23. The Slavocracy had been scared out of its wits by Toussaint Louverture's successful slave revolt on the island of Hispaniola.

Kentucky and Tennessee, were carved out of territory previously claimed by Virginia and North Carolina. Almost all of the settlers were natives from those two states, and many had brought their slaves with them. Kentucky and Tennessee were admitted as new slave states in 1792 and 1796, the only alternative being to deny them admission to the Union.

In the Northwest Territory, many of the initial settlers were from Virginia and later Kentucky, and despite Article VI of the Northwest Ordinance, by the time of Ohio's admission to the Union as a free state in 1800, slavery was entrenched in much of the rest of the territory. As early as 1788, the territorial agent for the area that later became the states of Illinois and Indiana, asked Congress to modify the Northwest Ordinance to allow slavery, and his report was endorsed by James Madison. In 1802, a convention of settlers meeting at Vincennes, presided over by future President William Henry Harrison, asked Congress to repeal Article VI; and in 1806 the territory adopted a new law aptly titled "An Act concerning Slaves and Servants." This was nothing less than a full slave code. During this entire period, leading up to the admission of Illinois as a "free state" in 1818, not one action was taken in the Territory to free the slaves in the region. After 1803, under Virginia native and territorial Governor Harrison, slavery began to actually expand in the territory, and this continued after statehood. When Illinois applied for admission to the Union in 1818, DeWitt Clinton protégé James Tallmadge of New York fiercely opposed statehood, based on the fact that slavery was still rampant in the territory. Not until 1848, when Illinois adopted a new State Constitution, was slavery officially abolished in Illinois.

The Louisiana Purchase was the golden opportunity to put Jefferson's "defusion" scheme into practice. Many Federalist Party leaders opposed the Louisiana Purchase, but Hamilton and Morris were not among them. Morris wrote a letter of congratulation to his old friend Robert Livingston, and both he and Hamilton spoke out praising what this would mean for the future of the nation. But the New Yorkers were also keenly aware of the potential grave danger, and Morris and Jay both insisted that as the vast new territory was "federal land," not previously part of, or claimed by, any pre-existing state—unlike Tennessee and Kentucky—that the anti-slavery principle of the Northwest Ordinance must be imposed on the new territory. Morris in particu-

lar spoke frequently and vehemently on this theme.[24] It was to no avail. With Jefferson and Madison running the country, settlers from Virginia, Georgia, the Carolinas and Kentucky poured across the Mississippi River, and with them came their slaves. New Orleans was quickly transformed into the slave hub of the South,[25] and the State of Louisiana was admitted as a slave state in 1812, under Madison.

Following the War of 1812, the Slave Power land grab became an avalanche. Mississippi and Alabama, which were formed on land partially seized from Spain, were admitted as slave states in 1817 and 1819; Arkansas constituted as a slave Territory in 1819;[26] Missouri was admitted as a slave state in 1821; and in 1822, Florida was organized as a slave territory. In a mere ten years, from 1812 to 1822—under the Virginians Madison and Monroe—341,000 square miles of new territory had been brought under the control of the Slave Power.

This was the intent all along. To crush the republic of Hamilton and his allies and replace it with a Slavocracy—this was the goal of Jefferson, Madison and Monroe from no later than 1789 and probably earlier. In 1800, almost half the slaves in the United States were in Virginia. Another 35 percent were in Maryland and the Carolinas. That is the actual Jeffersonian "republican" movement.

Missouri and Afterwards

In 1819 the first move was made to spread the electoral power of the Slavocracy northward up the Mississippi River. Henry Clay supported it. Thomas Jefferson supported it. President Monroe stated publicly that he would veto any bill which admitted Missouri as a "free" state. After 18 years in power, the South was prepared

---

24. Morris served in the U.S. Senate from 1800 to 1803. In 1801 he attempted to ban the importation of slaves into the Mississippi Territory, and in 1803 he authored a bill to prohibit the creation of any new Slave states in the new Louisiana Territory. He was defeated in both efforts.

25. Prior to 1803 there were a sizable number of free blacks and Creoles in New Orleans. After the United States took control, efforts were made to re-enslave these individuals. In 1811 the largest slave revolt in U.S. History, the Louisiana German Coast Uprising, was brutally suppressed, and slavery was ruthlessly enforced.

26. There was fierce opposition to approving the pro-slavery territorial constitution of Arkansas, and Congress deadlocked in their vote. Henry Clay personally fought for the pro-slavery territorial constitution (the first ever allowed in the Louisiana Territory) and cast the tie-breaking vote to allow slavery in Arkansas.

to make its move.

Eventually, as most Americans know, Henry Clay's Missouri Compromise brought in Missouri as a slave state, and supposedly secured peace between the North and South for the next 30 years. But remnants of Washington's New Yorkers, now fewer in numbers and politically weakened, saw things differently. John Jay, the last still-living member of Washington's inner circle, came out of retirement and denounced Clay's plan as a plot to spread slavery, as did Elias Boudinot, Hamilton's former partner in the Society for Useful Manufactures. In the Congress, a

Rufus King, in an 1820 portrait by Gilbert Stuart

fierce fight was launched in both houses to block the admission of Missouri as a slave state. This was led by two New Yorkers. In the Senate, Hamilton's friend Rufus King (still a Federalist), the last signer of the U.S. Constitution still serving in the Senate, single-handedly took on the Slave Interest, and he was joined, in the House of Representatives, by New Yorker and DeWitt Clinton protégé James Tallmadge (a Democrat-Republican). Tallmadge almost succeeded. His Tallmadge Amendment of 1819, which would have abolished slavery in Missouri, passed the House of Representatives on February 16, 1819, despite Henry Clay's opposition, but was then defeated in the Senate.

In the Senate, Rufus King delivered two speeches strongly opposing Missouri's admission as a slave state. These speeches infuriated Jefferson, Madison and Monroe. (Monroe had hated King for years.) John Quincy Adams states in his Diary that the Slaveholders in the Senate who listened to King, "gnawed their lips and clenched their fists in anger." King's two speeches paraphrased,—almost directly quoted,—Gouverneur Morris's anti-slavery speeches from the Constitutional Convention, particularly his attacks on the Three-Fifths clause. Later, in his 1860 Cooper Union address, Abraham Lincoln would name King twice, for his authorship of the anti-slavery Article VI of the Northwest Ordinance, and for his opposition to the Missouri Compromise, as an example of a founding father who opposed the spread of slavery into the territories.

Many people who recognized the evil of Missouri's admission as a slave state, individuals who should have spoken out, did nothing. Mathew Carey was silent. Carey's ally, the anti-slavery Hezekiah Niles, wrote to Carey saying, "I am rather discouraged, but frightened not. The Southern influence rules, and that is hostile to free white labor. It is great in its means, indefatigable in its exertions and united. It must be put down, or in my honest opinion, the country will literally be beggared,"—but publicly Niles endorsed the Compromise and uttered not one word of criticism of Monroe or Clay. Perhaps the most conflicted individual was John Quincy Adams, who wrote admiringly of Rufus King's stand in the United States Senate; and when Congress passed the Missouri Enabling Act, Adams wrote, "Take it for granted that the present is a mere preamble—a title page to a great, tragic volume,"—yet Adams would not break with Monroe and the Virginia combine in 1820, and he publicly endorsed the Compromise and lobbied in Congress for its passage.[27]

Contrary to most high-school history books, the issue of slavery did not fade into the background after the Missouri Compromise. Slaveowners and their "property" continued to pour up the Mississippi River and into the West. Arkansas was admitted as a slave state in 1836 and Florida in early 1845. In late 1845, Texas was admitted as a slave state, an action which both John Quincy Adams and Abraham Lincoln opposed as a massive expansion of the Slave Power. After the war with Mexico, the South connived to bring all of the newly acquired possessions into the Union as slave territory, including intensive nearly-successful efforts to bring in both California and Oregon as slave states.

When, in 1849, David Wilmot, a Northern congress-

---

27. Adams' later heroic battle against the Slave Power in the House of Representatives is well known, so there is no need to discuss it here. Clearly, by the 1830s, Adams recognized the enemy and was determined to stand against it.

man, proposed an amendment preventing the extension of slavery into any of the territory gained from Mexico,[28] the aging Henry Clay (now with the support of Stephen Douglas) acted for the Slave Power once again, this time with the Compromise of 1850, which allowed the expansion of slavery into the entire southwest (Arizona, New Mexico and Utah), legalized the interstate slave trade, and imposed a brutal fugitive slave law.

Then came 1854, and victory for the Slave Power was within reach. Stephen Douglas' Kansas-Nebraska Act, with its provisions for "popular sovereignty," effectively legalized the introduction of slavery into all the territory west of the Mississippi River, as Jefferson and Madison had intended in 1803. With this act, the Whig Party, after a mere 20 years of appeasement to the Slave Power, vanished. Three years later, the Dred Scott Decision *de facto* opened up the entire nation, including the Northeast, to slavery.

There are many, past and present, who defend the compromises of 1820 and 1850, proclaiming that they were the only way to prevent a break-up of the Union. As we now know, despite the "compromises" the Union did break up, and when that came in 1861 it was terrible. What almost everyone fails to recognize, is that the South never wanted to "be left alone;" that it was never the case that as long as no one interfered with their "peculiar institution" of human bondage, they would peacefully co-exist with the North. From the beginning, it was the design of the Virginia Slave Power to take over and dominate the entire nation, and over a span of 70 years their efforts were unceasing and relentless.

---

28. This Amendment, known today is the Wilmot Proviso, was modeled on Rufus King's Northwest Ordinance. Like the Tallmadge Amendment from 30 years earlier, it passed the House of Representatives and stood a good chance of enactment before Henry Clay intervened to kill it.

FIGURE 1:
The Mississipi/Missouri River System

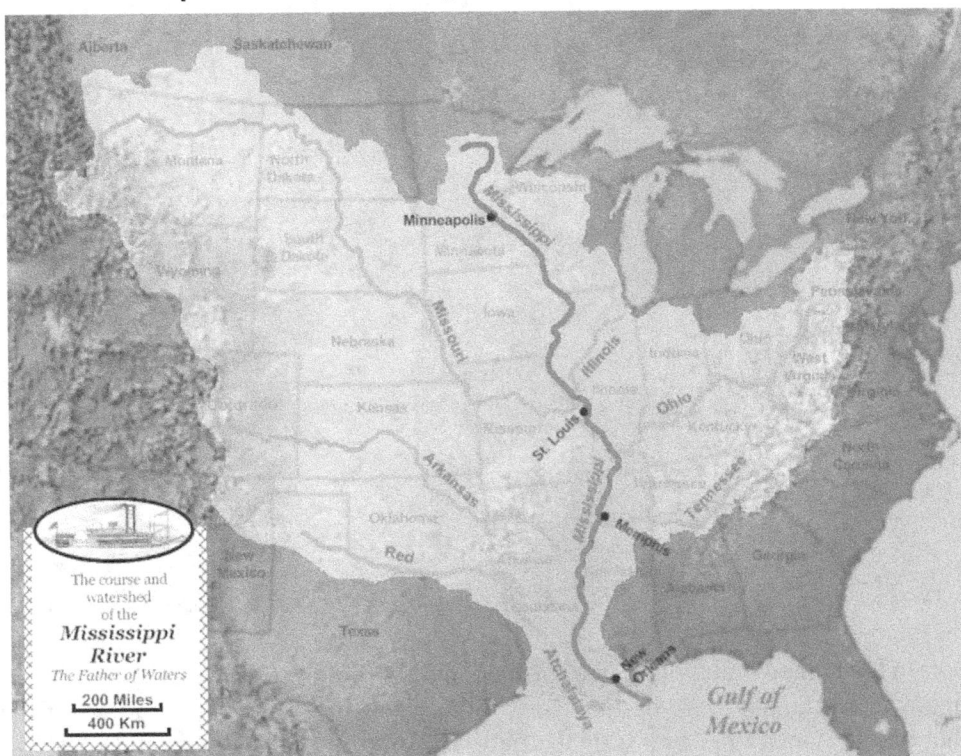

Part V
The Erie Canal & DeWitt Clinton

First, let us discuss the Erie Canal from the standpoint of the war between Hamilton's New Yorkers and the Slave Power. Then we will look at a little of its history and other implications.

Look at two maps. First, a map of the Mississippi-Arkansas-Ohio-Missouri River system (**Figure 1**). From New Orleans the Mississippi River stretches up through Arkansas, Missouri, Illinois, Iowa, Wisconsin, and into Minnesota. Of its three main tributaries, the Arkansas River reaches out to Kansas, Oklahoma and Colorado; the Missouri River flows north to Nebraska, South Dakota and Montana; and the great Ohio River extends eastward into Kentucky, Ohio, Indiana, Pennsylvania, and western New York State. It is a river basin that covers 50 percent of the total land mass of the continental United States.

After 1803 it became the intention of the Virginia Slave Power to transform New Orleans into the largest

FIGURE 2
The Great Lakes Region

port in the United States, as well as the commercial and financial capital of a slave-dominated economic system that would control the future of the nation. New Orleans would become the entry-point into a vast inland slave territory, with commercial goods coming down the river and slavery spreading up the river.

Next look at a map of the Great Lakes region, with New York City as the easternmost point (**Figure 2**). This covers an area stretching from Manhattan, out through Buffalo to Pennsylvania, Ohio, Michigan, Illinois, Indiana, Wisconsin and Minnesota. The Erie Canal was intended to direct all of the commerce of this region through New York, as well as to enable the settlement of these new regions by free New Yorkers and New Englanders.

Furthermore, a second canal—the Ohio & Erie Canal—was constructed in tandem with the Erie Canal through the collaboration of DeWitt Clinton and Ohio Governor Thomas Worthington. It linked Lake Erie to the Ohio River, thus allowing all the traffic from that river to travel eastward to New York City.

The Erie Canal was a strategic flank (attack) on the Slave Power. And it was understood to be so by Gouverneur Morris. The issue was "who would control the westward expansion of the nation." Morris, Jay, and most emphatically Hamilton, before his death, were determined to make New York City the commercial, cultural, and political capital of the Republic. By 1803,

Morris viewed the Erie Canal project as a life-and-death strategic necessity to prevent the takeover of the nation by the Slave Power.[29]

Morris and Clinton

If one had to bestow the title of "Father of the Erie Canal" on any one person, that honor most certainly would have to be given to Gouverneur Morris. He was the first to propose the canal, in 1777, and after his return from Europe in 1797, the Erie Canal project consumed most of the rest of his life. In 1800 Morris drafted detailed plans for a canal to Lake Erie which he submitted to New York Surveyor General Simeon DeWitt. At the time DeWitt dismissed the plan as impractical, but years later he would write: The merit of first starting the idea of a direct communication by water between Lake Erie and the Hudson River unquestionably belongs to Gouverneur Morris."

In 1801, Morris toured the region, from Albany to Lakes Ontario and Erie and Niagara Falls, exploring the topology and the obstacles to a future canal.

Between 1800 and 1808, Morris wrote letters, lobbied in Albany, and propagandized for the Canal. In 1809 he traveled to Washington D.C. and testified before a special Committee in the House of Representatives, requesting (unsuccessfully) that the National Government undertake and finance the Canal project. In 1810, DeWitt Clinton, who had been working with Morris since 1807 on Morris's design to transform Manhattan Island, came on board the campaign to build the Canal.

---

29. A tributary project to the strategic Canal Initiative was the Blueprint for New York City, devised by Gouverneur Morris between 1807 and 1811. Morris headed a five man committee and employed the same engineers and surveyors involved in the Erie Canal Project. The result was the famous Manhattan "Grid" of avenues and streets from Houston Street in the South to Harlem in the North. Manhattan is essentially man-made (or Morris-made), as hills were flattened, dales leveled, swamps filled, and forests cleared. This was done in tandem with the Erie Canal Project to prepare New York to become the economic and political driver of the nation upon the Canal's completion.

In 1810, at Morris's request, the New York legislature appointed a seven-person "Commission to Explore a Route for a Canal to Lake Erie," which became known as the Erie Canal Commission. Gouverneur Morris was selected first, Steven Van Rensselaer second, and DeWitt Clinton third. For the next five years, Morris served as Chairman of the Commission.[30] During the summer of 1810, the entire Commission would spend two months in western New York exploring possible routes for the Canal.

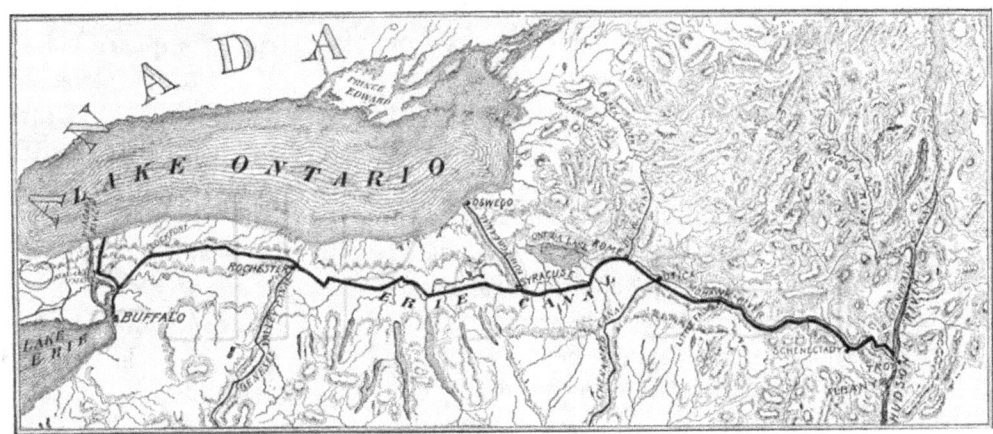

FIGURE 3
The Erie Canal, c. 1840

In 1811, Morris and Clinton, now joined by Robert Fulton (whose steamboat had been launched on the Hudson River four years earlier), launched an all-out campaign for the Canal, criss-crossing the state and speaking at numerous public events to organize support. As part of the campaign, Clinton authors the "Atticus" letters, which appear in the *New York Evening Post* to popularize the project, and in January of 1812, Morris and Clinton make a second trip to Washington D.C., which this time includes a meeting with President Madison. Madison turns down their request for aid, stating that it would be unconstitutional to finance such a project.

Finally, following the submission of an extensive report, authored by Morris, to the New York Legislature, in June of 1812 the Legislature authorizes the Commission to borrow $5 million to begin work on the canal. Within weeks engineering studies begin.

And that is where the project almost died. Less than one month after the New York vote, the United States declared war on Great Britain, and over the next two and one-half years, funding dried up and political support evaporated. In 1814, the Legislature repealed the 1812 Act which had authorized the Canal construction, and by 1815 the project was dead. But on December 31, 1815, Morris, Clinton, and the other commissioners meet with 100 potential financial backers in New York City, and present a detailed plan, at an estimated cost of $6 million, with a completion timetable of ten to fifteen years. Public meetings are organized throughout the Hudson and Mohawk Valleys to explain the plan and organize support, and in early 1816, a petition, signed by tens of thousands throughout the state, is presented to the Legislature, stating that a completed canal will "convey more riches on its waters than any other canal in the world."

In April, a new Commission is selected, now headed by Clinton and including Stephen Van Rensselaer, and in 1817 a New Canal Bill authorizes the beginning of construction, which starts at Rome, New York on July 4.

It would take eight years to complete, but when finished there was nothing like it anywhere. At 353 miles, it was by far the world's longest man-made waterway, with 83 locks and 17 aqueducts. Its construction overcame staggering natural obstacles.

It could not have happened without DeWitt Clinton.[31] He was attacked every step of the way by the political machine of the Slavocracy-allied Martin Van Buren, who at one point even had him thrown off the Canal Commission, and throughout the entire period, no one in the Monroe Administration would lift a finger to help (Monroe despised Clinton). But year-in and year-out he fought, and in 1824, running against the Democratic-Republican Party, he was elected Governor on the ticket of the People's Party, and by 1825 the Canal was completed. Here is a description of what followed:

---

30. Later Chairmen of the Erie Canal Commission would include DeWitt Clinton, Steven Van Rensselaer and John Jay's son Peter Jay. Future Directors of the Commission included Alexander Hamilton's nephew Philip Schuyler Church and Rufus King's son Edward.

31. Gouverneur Morris had died in 1816.

October 26—In Buffalo thousands gather, entertained by a military band, booming cannons, and speeches, followed by a 5,000-person parade, led by Governor Clinton, through the streets of Buffalo. At 10:00 a.m., the Seneca Chief enters the canal at Buffalo, heading east for Albany. Celebrations ensue along the canal route at major towns and cities, with fireworks, rifle volleys from the local militia, and even the launching of a balloon. A Cannon Volley was organized along the route, with cities along the canal and Hudson River participating. It began in Buffalo, and it was organized so that the next nearest city could hear the first blast. When the blast from Buffalo died out, the next city on the route fired its cannons, and then the next one after that all the way to Albany and then down the Hudson River to New York City. Then it went in reverse, up the Hudson and west on the Canal to Buffalo. The completed round trip of cannon volleys took 160 minutes. Governor Clinton heads a delegation which makes the complete inaugural trip from Buffalo to New York. At Albany the flotilla of boats is tied together and pulled by a steamboat down the Hudson to New York City. On November 4th, the Seneca Chief arrives at New York harbor at 7:00 a.m., followed by the Wedding of the Waters ceremony, in which a keg of Lake Erie water is emptied into the Atlantic at Sandy Hook.

Within five years of the Canal's opening, Buffalo became the busiest lakeport in the United States, and between 1830 and 1850 more Americans emigrated to the west (via the Great Lakes) through the Erie Canal than by any other land or sea-based route. Manhattan was now the gateway to the nation's heartland.

1812

By 1812 there were two surviving members of Washington's 1789 New York inner circle still alive—John Jay and Gouverneur Morris. Additionally, Washington's two closest Virginia friends—John Marshall and Henry Lee[32]—were also still alive, as were several others who had been closely associated with the first Washington Administration, such as Rufus King. All of these people, every single one of them, opposed—**strongly opposed**—the War of 1812.

That reality alone should cause one to stop and reflect. That War was bitterly opposed and denounced by every individual who had been closely allied with George Washington between 1789 and 1797—among whom were Alexander Hamilton's most intimate friends and associates. You can not shrug this off, or ignore it.

Not surprisingly, Morris was the most vocal and the least cautious in his attacks, and Morris placed the responsibility for the war squarely at the feet of the Slave Power. Morris charged, repeatedly and publicly, that the war was pushed through by the slave states for the purpose of vastly expanding their power over the nation. In a letter to Rufus King, Morris blamed the Three-Fifths clause of the Constitution as the ultimate *casus belli*, and stated that the war was all about "strangling commerce, whipping Negroes, and bawling about the inborn and inalienable rights of man." Later, after the fighting had begun, he declared "If Peace be not immediately made with England, the Question on Negro votes [i.e., the Three-Fifths clause] must divide the Union."

More will be said below on the causes and outcome of the War, but for now, consider the following:

In June 1812, the U.S. House of Representatives voted 79 to 49 to declare war against Britain; the Senate voted 19 to 13 for war, for a combined Congressional vote of 98 to 62. This is by far—nothing else even comes close—the strongest Congressional opposition to a declaration of war in American History.[33]

One myth insists that the opposition to the War came solely from traitorous pro-British New England Federalists (who admittedly existed), but even a cursory examination of the Congressional vote provides a different picture. In the Senate the vote was 19 to 13 for war. The pro-war 19 included 12 Senators from slave states and 4 from free states. *All 10 Senators representing a state which later joined the Confederacy in 1861 (Virginia, North Carolina, South Carolina, Georgia and Tennessee) voted for the war.* The 13 anti-war votes included 9 from free states and 4 from slave states. The

---

32. Henry "Lighthorse Harry" Lee is often derided by historians as the father of Robert E. Lee (which he was), but he was, perhaps, the only member of the extended Lee clan of Virginia not in service to the Slave Power. He was trusted by Hamilton, personally both close and intensely loyal to Washington, and he delivered the eulogy at Washington's fu-

neral, uttering the words, "First in War, first in Peace, and first in the Hearts of his Countrymen." For opposing the War of 1812 Lee was beaten nearly to death by a Jeffersonian mob in Baltimore.

33. The next closest vote was the U.S. Senate's Declaration of War against Germany in 1917 by a vote of 82 to 6.

majority of the 13 anti-war Senate votes were cast not by Federalists (who only had 6 Senators) but by Democratic-Republicans, most of them backers of DeWitt Clinton, including **both** New York Senators, Clinton Democrats who voted against the Declaration of War. Another of the anti-war votes came from the Clinton-allied Ohio Senator Thomas Worthington, later famous as "the Father of the Ohio-Erie Canal."[34]

The Battle of Baltimore, 1814

The leading anti-war Democrat in the Senate was Obadiah German of New York, a DeWitt Clinton loyalist. The general view of the Clintonians was that the correct path was, first, to massively upgrade the military capabilities of the nation, something DeWitt Clinton had been calling for since 1808,—and then to intensify the negotiations with both Britain and France, but from a position of military strength. Senator German declared, "A country well-prepared to meet war will scarcely find war necessary, but if it cannot be avoided, preparation does away with half its terrors," and "as to the great object of our wishes, an adjustment of our differences with Great Britain, I have never entertained a doubt that it might have been effected in a satisfactory manner long before the declaration of war, had our Executive entertained just and proper dispositions in regard to it."

Senator German also posited that it was in Georgia and South Carolina that were to be found "the combustibles that have ignited this mighty war flame, and precipitated this nation to the verge of ruin." German went on to charge that it was Crawford of Georgia in the Senate, and Calhoun of South Carolina in the House, who were leading the nation into war.

In Pennsylvania, both Senators, the Democrat-Republicans Leib and Gregg—although they ultimately voted for the final declaration of war—did everything in their power to prevent the war declaration from coming to a vote, through numerous maneuvers and repeated attempts to limit the scope of the war. During and after these efforts Senator Leib, a protégé of Benjamin Franklin, was widely and publicly criticized on the floor of Congress and by pro-Madison newspapers as a "Clintonian."

In the House of Representatives, the proportional breakdown of the vote between free and slave states was almost identical to that in the Senate, and it must be pointed out that in 1812, there were over 1 million slaves in the South, which under the Three-Fifths clause greatly inflated the voting strength of the slave states. Of the 107 Democratic-Republican members of the House of Representatives, 52 were from slave states and 55 from free states. Among the 55 Democratic-Republican representatives from free states, half of them (50 percent) either voted against the war or abstained from voting. The Southern delegates voted overwhelmingly for war. **Twelve of New York's fifteen representatives voted against the declaration of war, almost evenly divided between Federalists and Clinton Democrats.**

Additionally, if you look at the Congressional leaders who between 1810 and 1812 were agitating the most aggressively for war, almost all of them were representatives of the Slave Power, including:

Henry Clay (Kentucky), John C. Calhoun (South Carolina), William Crawford (Georgia), William Carey Nicholas (Virginia), George Washington Campbell (Tennessee), Joseph Desha (Kentucky), Felix Grundy (Tennessee), Richard Mentor Johnson (Kentucky), William Lowndes (South Carolina), Langdon Cheves (South Carolina), and William W. Bibb (Georgia). There were, admittedly, other strong war supporters, such as Jonathan Roberts from Pennsylvania, but by-and-large the "war hawks" were agents of the Slavocracy. Sometimes this Southern role is obfuscated by

---

34. Worthington was also the legal guardian of Rufus King's son Edward, and Edward King would marry Worthington's daughter.

claiming that it was the new republican "Western" influence in the nation which rallied the country against the British in 1812,[35] but between 1789 and 1812 only three "western" states had been admitted to the Union, and two of them—Kentucky and Tennessee—were slave states. During the war, Louisiana would also be admitted as a state, so that by 1814, six of the eight Senators "from the West" were representatives of the Slave Power.

Causes and Effects

The notion that the impressment of American sailors by the British was the trigger for the War of 1812, is a falsified myth created later as part of the legend of the "Second War for Independence." The truth about the practice of "impressment" is that it was legal, its legality was recognized by every United States Administration (Washington, Adams, Jefferson, Madison, Monroe),[36] and it was practiced by all of the European empires, British, French, Dutch, Spanish and Portuguese. The involuntary seizing of idle or otherwise-occupied sailors for service into an empire's navy was seen as the "military draft" of its day. Conflict arose with Britain only because in "impressing" British subjects serving aboard U.S. vessels, a substantial number of U.S. citizens were also being seized. But there are two things to keep in mind. At no time in 1812 did Madison, Monroe, Clay or anyone else name "impressment" as the reason to go to war; and secondly, the policy of impressment was so important to the British Royal fleet, that the United States was never able to get the British to sign a treaty outlawing the practice: not in 1783, not with the Jay Treaty, not with the Monroe-Pinckney Treaty, and not with the Treaty of Ghent in 1815. At the end of the War of 1812 the policy of impressment was still being conducted, and the United States government agreed to that.

At the onset of the war, in 1812, the key British "provocation" which was put forward by the "war hawks" as the *casus belli*, was the 1806 issuance by the British Government of what was called an "Order in Council," which declared the entire coast of France and northern Europe under blockade. In 1807 the blockade was extended to the entire European continent, and all goods and ships which violated this blockade could be seized as contraband. Dozens of U.S. vessels were seized and tons of merchandise confiscated. However, the British Order in Council was actually promulgated in response to the slightly earlier Berlin Decree of Napoleon, which he then followed with the 1807 Milan Decree, declaring Britain under blockade and stating that any ships found honoring the British blockade were also liable to seizure. After 1807 all American shipping was open to seizure by the British, French or both, and both nations harassed American shipping with equal ferocity.

As many pointed out at the time, practically all of the issues of conflict with Britain could have been resolved if Jefferson had signed the 1806 Monroe-Pinckney Treaty, but in 1807 Jefferson rejected the Treaty (negotiated by his own representatives) because of its close resemblance to the 1795 Jay Treaty.

In November of 1810, President Madison issued a

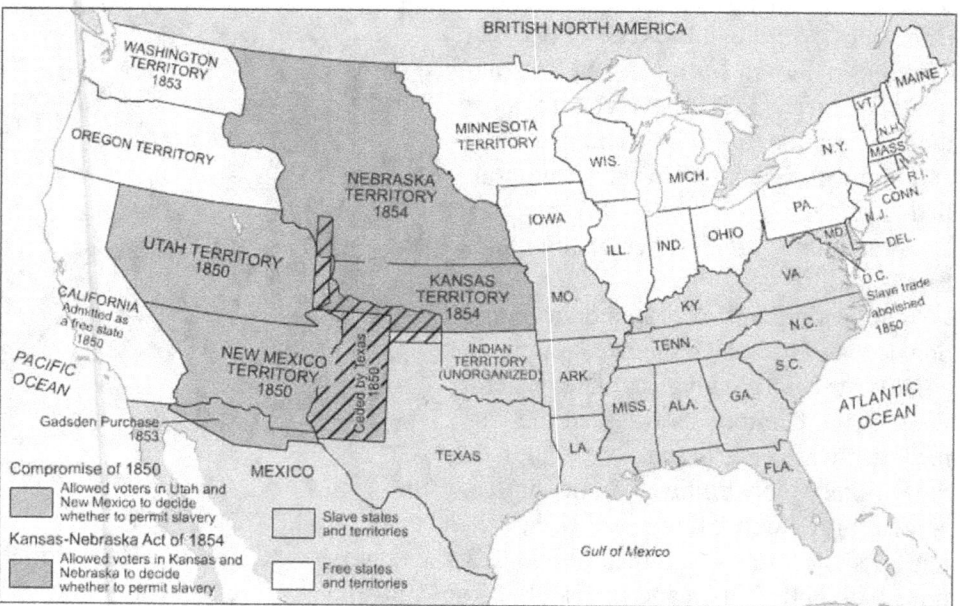

FIGURE 4
What the Slavocracy Wrought

---

35. As if somehow, magically, being from "the West" confers the status of Guardian of the Republic.

36. None of these Administrations ever objected to the impressment of British subjects from American vessels, since British subjects came under British law.

statement that Napoleon had revoked the Berlin and Milan decrees—which was completely false—and Madison gave Britain an ultimatum to remove all trade restrictions within three months or face retaliation. Even after France continued to seize U.S. shipping, and it became apparent that the Berlin and Milan Decrees were still in effect, from January of 1811 onward, the political escalation for war with Britain became unstoppable.

One irony in the Chain of Events, is that the British eventually did repeal the entirety of the Orders in Council on June 23, 1812, but news of the repeal did not reach America for six weeks, and by then Madison had signed the Declaration of War on July 25th. After news of the British action reached Washington D.C.— and prior to any actual fighting between the belligerents— Madison and Monroe both admitted that there was no reason to continue the war; there was, in effect, nothing to fight about.

This failure by the United States to define actual, legitimate war aims, was later reflected in the 1815 Treaty of Ghent. Negotiated by Henry Clay, Albert Gallatin, and John Quincy Adams, the treaty returned relations to the 1812 pre-war status quo. Boundaries were restored, trade polices remained unchanged, impressment of seamen went unmentioned and continued. The U.S.A. achieved **NONE** of its supposed war aims, which were very unclear to begin with. The British agreed to **only one** concession: that they would reimburse the United States $1,204,960 in compensation for the slaves they had captured and freed during the war. So the slaveowners were paid.

After reading the treaty, Rufus King stated that the document "is scarcely worth the wax of its Seals..., and leaves every point of Dispute and disagreement unsettled."

Gouverneur Morris described the war as "rashly declared, prodigally maintained, weakly conducted, and meanly concluded."

One thing that did emerge out of the war was the expansion of the Slave Power. Mississippi and Alabama were soon admitted as slave states (following Louisiana), and in 1813 Madison authorized a military invasion and occupation of Spanish Florida, a nation with which we were not at war,—eventually leading to the establishment of Florida as a Slave Territory under Andrew Jackson in 1818.

Later, as part of the effort to mythologize the war as the "Second American Revolution," it was declaimed that the main accomplishment of the war was somehow linked to its effect on the National Psyche, i.e., that the nation emerged from the war with "a renewed sense of self-reliance and common national identity,"—as if previously we had been suffering from some sort of a lack of national identity or an inferiority complex vis-à-vis Great Britain. Let me assure you that George Washington, Alexander Hamilton and Gouverneur Morris had no "inferiority complex" as concerns Britain, nor were they confused about the nature of the American Republic.

One example of this rhetoric is an 1815 letter that pro-war Pennsylvania Congressman Jonathan Roberts wrote to his brother, wherein —after first admitting that none of the pre-war aims had been achieved—he goes on to proclaim that "Victory perches on our banner ... the triumph over Aristocrats and Monarchists is equally glorious with that over the enemy—it is the triumph of virtue over vice, of republican men and republican principles over the advocates and doctrines of Tyranny."

Really! Is that what the war was about? Triumph over the alleged advocates of monarchy and aristocracy inside the United States? As Gouverneur Morris had identified as early as the 1787 Philadelphia Convention, there was only one truly evil aristocracy inside the United States, and it was headquartered in the South.

At this point, I will propose a—perhaps unfair—hypothetical question to the reader: What would Alexander Hamilton and George Washington have done? Had they been alive in 1812, what would they have done? It is worth considering.

Clinton vs. Madison

On May 18, 1812 the Democratic-Republican National Caucus nominated James Madison for a second term as President of the United States. Ten days later, the New York Democratic-Republican Party, meeting in Manhattan, nominated DeWitt Clinton for President. On July 25th the United States declared war on Britain, and eleven days later, on August Fifth, Gouverneur Morris invited John Jay, Rufus King, and DeWitt Clinton to his home in New York City. At the meeting Morris proposed that they join together to prevent the Federalists from running a presidential campaign, and throw their support behind DeWitt Clinton. King refuses to endorse Clinton, but Jay and Clinton agree and a "fusion" ticket between Clinton's Democrats and what was left of the old Washington New York leadership is born. In reply to a challenge from King as to his motives, Clinton vows that he "was separated from the administration forever; that he pledged his honor that the Breach was irreparable."

Morris sends an invitation to Federalist Party leaders

throughout the nation, inviting them to attend an emergency meeting in Manhattan. For three days, from September Fifteenth through Seventeenth, sixty Federalist Party leaders meet in New York City. The discussions are contentious, but at the end, under Morris's influence, they agree not to run a Presidential candidate, but to unofficially and privately back Clinton. At one point, a group of Federalist leaders proposes the nomination of John Marshall, but Marshall demurs, endorsing the fusion ticket with Clinton. Only Rufus King and one or two others dissent. (In the election, the Federalist Party, with King as their nominee, appeared on the ballot in only one state, Virginia.) For the next seven weeks the national Clinton campaign is run out of an office in Manhattan by Clinton, Morris, and a mixture of Federalists and Democrats.

This was a bi-partisan challenge to the Virginia Combine. For example, an editorial in the *Cooperstown Federalist* read:

DeWitt Clinton, by Rembrandt Peale

> This nomination speaks a language that will not be misunderstood anywhere; and in our humble opinion, will tend more to lower the proud crest of the lordly Virginians than any measure which has been adopted since the election of Mr. Jefferson to the Presidency—The people of all parties in the Northern and Eastern sections of the Union have had their eyes opened by that ruinous system of measures which has been pursued for the last ten years; by a government pretending to be the friends of the people but in reality their worst enemies. ... It must rejoice the heart of every good man, of every friend to his country, to find that the democratic-republicans of the FIRST STATE OF THE UNION, have dared to make a stand against the usurpation and overbearing aristocracy of Virginia."

To understand how these extraordinary events transpired, it is necessary to go back two years to the creation of the Erie Canal Commission. At that time Federalists and Democratic-Republicans were at each others' throats. The term "bitter enemies" would be an understatement. Yet Gouverneur Morris and DeWitt Clinton formed a personal alliance, around which they consciously created a bi-partisan political movement. Like-minded Federalists and Democrats were recruited to one of the greatest projects in mankind's history, a design to transform the entire nation. In essence, the Erie Canal Project gave birth to the Clinton Presidential candidacy. It is very possible (hypothetically) that the decision for the campaign might have occurred in January of 1812, when Morris and Clinton traveled to Washington DC, and Madison told them to their faces that they would not receive one penny to construct the Canal. Whatever the actual chronology, it was the Canal—*and what it represented as a means to break the grip of the Virginia Slave Power*—which was at the heart of the Clinton-Morris relationship.

There were other contributing factors as well, including the effort by a cross-party alliance of Federalists and Clinton Democrats in the spring of 1812, following the 1811 abolition of Hamilton's National Bank, to charter the $6 million Bank of America in New York City, which was seen as a means for transferring the financial center of the nation from Philadelphia back to New York. This was vetoed by Madison-allied New York Governor Daniel Tompkins.

Clinton's campaign was anti-war but not "peacenik." He campaigned on the same theme as had been expressed by many of his allies in Congress. That the war was ruinous, divisive, and unnecessary, and should be concluded honorably as soon as possible. At the same time, the nation's economic strength and military capability should be rebuilt, so that in the future, negotiations with Britain, France, Spain and other European empires might be conducted from a position of strength.

In the end Clinton lost the presidential election to Madison by only 7,600 votes in the popular vote. Every state north of the Delaware River except Vermont went for Clinton. All of the slave states voted for Madison (although Clinton received a fraction of the electoral votes in the border states of Delaware and Maryland). The deciding state was Pennsylvania, whose electoral votes gave Madison the election.[37] This subservience to the slave interests would continue for some years to come, with Pennsylvania voting for Monroe in 1816 and 1820, and then voting overwhelmingly for Andrew Jackson (over John Quincy Adams) in both 1824 and 1828.

---

37. Madison actually suffered huge vote losses in Pennsylvania, particularly in the west, from his 1808 totals. What secured him victory was the continued romance between the Philadelphia clubs and the Virginia slave-owners, combined with an incredible deal whereby the U.S. government allowed all of the eastern Pennsylvania grain farmers to sell their flour to the British (!) army with the stipulation that the British would agree to use the flour only to feed soldiers fighting Napoleon and not soldiers fighting the United States!

If the Three-Fifths clause had not been in effect, it is very possible that Clinton would have won the election, even without Pennsylvania. There is no exact way to compute the figures, but is certainly the case that without the "slave electors" Madison would have received 30 or 40 fewer electoral votes, and the election could have gone either way.

Part VI
Into the Future

The mystic chords of memory, stretching from every battlefield and patriot grave to every living heart and hearthstone all over this broad land, will yet swell the chorus of the Union, when again touched, as surely they will be, by the better angels of our nature.

Abraham Lincoln, First Inaugural Address

'An Asylum to Mankind'

"The portals of the Temple we have raised to Freedom, shall then be thrown wide, as an Asylum to mankind. America shall receive to her bosom and comfort and cheer the oppressed, the miserable and the poor of every nation and of every clime. The enterprise of extending commerce shall wave her friendly flag over the billows of the remotest region of the world. We shall learn to consider all men as our brethren, being equally children of the Universal Parent—that God of the heavens and of the earth, whose infinite Majesty, for providential favour during the late revolution, almighty power in our preservation from impending ruin, and gracious mercy in our redemption from the iron shackles of despotism, we cannot cease with gratitude and with deep humility to praise, to reverence and adore."

—Gouverneur Morris, 1778
"Observations on the American Revolution"

A few weeks before his death, Gouverneur Morris wrote, in an open letter to leaders of the Federalist Party: "Gentlemen, let us forget party and think of our country. That country embraces both parties. We must endeavor, therefore, to save and benefit both.... Such *worthy* men may, I trust, be found in both parties; and if our country be delivered, what does it signify whether those who operate her salvation wear a federal or democratic cloak?... Perhaps the expression of these sentiments may be imprudent; but when it appears proper to speak the truth, I know not concealment. It has been the unvarying principle of my life, that the interest of our country must be preferred to every other interest."

Within days Morris would be dead. Through what leadership, and by what means could the words of his final political advice be accomplished? By 1816, all of the key New York leaders of Washington's first administration were gone. Although John Jay lived until 1829, he was in very poor health during the last twenty years of his life, and, except for two occasions—his opposition to the War of 1812 and his opposition to the Missouri Compromise— he remained in retirement from politics during that entire period. Rufus King lived until 1827, John Marshall until 1835 and Steven Van Rensselaer until 1839, but, despite the sometimes vital contributions of these individuals, the truth is that the promise of the Washington Administration died with Hamilton in 1804, and after the passing of Hamilton's partner Morris, the forces of the Slave Power controlled the nation. The obvious question was "What is to be done?"

Once again, the leadership in continuing the battle would emanate from New York, but before we turn to that story, there is one issue which must be disposed of.

Whence the Whigs?

In our discussion of the American Patriotic Tradition there has been no mention, until now, of the Whig Party. This has been deliberate.

The Whig Party, as a political party, was a deeply flawed institution, doomed to extinction from its moment of birth, and when the crises it had refused to address finally reached the point, in the 1850s, that the Nation itself faced dismemberment and ruin, that Party—lawfully—vanished, to be replaced by a new leadership, one founded on superior moral and philosophical principles. That new leadership was not the Republican Party, but the Lincoln Presidency.

There were several serious shortcomings in the Whig Party, but its horrendous, fatal flaw was its subservience to the Slave Power throughout its brief twenty years of existence. Let's be blunt about it. Henry Clay was a slave-owner, and he pushed to extend slavery into the territories until his dying breath. Despite his positive accomplishments, William Henry Harrison was also a slave-owner who fought to bring Illinois into the Union as a slave state. We all know what happened to John Calhoun.

This is not to say that there were not good—or even very good—people in the Whig Party, and the Whig Party was certainly a bastion of relative sanity when compared with the 1829-1841 Jackson and Van Buren Presidencies, but that was simply not adequate.

One insight into this problem can be found in the "ownership" which the Virginia Combine exercised over the Philadelphia Democratic-Republican Societies. Mathew Carey's Olive Branch is subtitled "Faults on Both Sides," and it purports to present an even-handed criticism of the Federalist and Jeffersonian parties. But there is one, huge, glaring omission. Nowhere in that document does Carey once mention slavery, and this *at a time when Gouverneur Morris and DeWitt Clinton were battling, by means of the Erie Canal Project, to break the grip of Virginia and the Slavocracy over the nation.* In every Presidential election from 1800 to 1820, a Virginian had been elected President and a New Yorker Vice-President.[38] The **strategic** battle led by Morris and Clinton was to shatter the Virginia supremacy and to make New York City the navigator for the Nation's Destiny. This battle was raging at the time the Olive Branch was published, but it simply does not appear in that document.

What of John Quincy Adams?, one might ask. First off, Adams was no Whig. He was his own Party; or, perhaps, one might say, in the words of Charles de Gaulle, that he used political parties "like taxi-cabs, to get to where he wanted to go." Adams went from being a Federalist, to a Democrat-Republican, to a National Republican, to a candidate of the Anti-Masonic Party,[39]

---

38. The Vice Presidents were Aaron Burr, the anti-Constitution George Clinton and Van Buren's man Daniel Tompkins.

39. A party founded in New York State after 1828 to rally those opposed to the new Presidency of Andrew Jackson. Thaddeus Stevens began his political career in the Anti-Masonic Party, and the 1832 Anti-Masonic Presidential Candidate William Wirt would lead the effort to prevent Andrew Jackson's extermination of the Cherokee Nation.

to a Whig, and during his post-1830 tenure in Congress, when he often stood alone against the Slave Power, he was out-of-step and shunned by the majority of the Whig leadership.

But there is more. The Whig Party is often seen as synonymous with Henry Clay's American System of Economics, as that "American System" is delineated in the three-point policy of: 1) a National Bank, 2) Internal Improvements, and 3) a high Protective Tariff.

That "American System," as enumerated above, is absolutely not the same thing as Alexander Hamilton's policy, nor is it coherent with the "Hamiltonian Principle," as Lyndon LaRouche has defined it.

First off—point by point—Hamilton actually vigorously *opposed* high protective tariffs. He considered them counterproductive to industrial and technological advancement, and injurious to trade. He supported a moderate tariff for revenue and to provide a modicum of protection to key parts of the economy. Secondly, on the National Bank, it must be understood that once Hamilton had left the Washington Administration, except for the brief 1825-1829 partnership between John Quincy Adams and Nicholas Biddle, neither the first nor the second National Bank ever functioned as a national Credit System in the way that Hamilton had intended. The issue was not the Bank, *per se*. A National Bank, yes; but for what purpose: to function as a mere monetary institution,— or as an engine for economic development?[40] The issue was one of intent. After Hamilton's death, the nation would not see a true Credit System until Lincoln's Greenback Policy of 1862.

This brings us to the issue of Internal Improvements, and there are two critically important things to consider. During the period from 1830 to 1850, many canals, roads and other important projects were built in the United States. Certainly, the Whig Party was more supportive of these projects than most of the Democrats. Yet,—and this is very important,— except for the Quincy Adams Presidency, between 1797 and 1861 there was never any *National* development policy, including under Monroe and the various Whig Presidents. Essentially, the policy of Internal Improve-

ments, as it was carried out during those years, has to be understood as a "States' Rights" internal improvement policy. Many good people did many good things, but it was the State Governments, or sometimes even private investors, who financed and built these projects, with practically no help or participation from the National Government. States were free to "do their own thing," but the hegemony of the Slave Power over the nation prevented any policy of unified National economic development. That Southern veto of a National policy was never seriously challenged by the Whigs.

But there is a more profound, axiomatic, aspect to this. The policy of "internal improvements," i.e. "infrastructure" in the form of canals, roads, ports, etc.,— as important and beneficial as these endeavors might be,—is absolutely *not* the same thing as a Hamiltonian "Science Driver" policy. It is extremely important to recognize that, during the first Washington Administration, the Virginia Combine, led by Jefferson, Madison and Monroe, were far more opposed to the policy intent contained in Hamilton's *Report on Manufactures*, than they were to his National Bank Proposal. In that Report, far from proposing a passive system of protectionism, Hamilton posited an active central role for the National government, including both his system of "bounties," as well as the way in which a National Credit System would be utilized, in defining how the National Government would consciously and deliberately direct the industrial and scientific advancement of the Nation. National productivity, science, cognitive and skill levels would all be advanced in such a way that this would become the very nature of the Republic itself. This outlook is not the same thing as "internal improvements," and for the Slave Power-influenced Whigs, such a Hamiltonian Principle was impossible to implement, because it stemmed from a vision of the nature of the human species, of the actual human identity, incompatible with the outlook of the Slavocracy.

The 1824 Election

First, DeWitt Clinton mounted an insurgent campaign, through the People's Party, for the New York Governorship, challenging the Van Buren-backed Democratic-Republican machine. Clinton's campaign became a referendum on his leadership in the Erie Canal Project, and Rufus King's son Charles

---

40. Gouverneur Morris actually opposed the re-chartering of the National Bank in 1815 because he considered the legislation incompetent, and he predicted that the new Bank would become a vehicle for unchecked speculation, leading to a financial crash, which is exactly what happened in the Panic of 1819.

joined the People's Party[41] and actively campaigned for Clinton. On election day, the voters overwhelming rejected the Van Buren state leadership and returned Canal-builder Clinton to office. At the same time, Rufus King publicly endorsed Adams and swung what was left of the Federalist Party base, still a significant though minority force in New York, behind the Adams campaign.[42] New York gave its electoral votes for Adams.

After the nationwide election failed to deliver a majority to any of the four candidates, the choice for a new President was given to the House of Representatives, where it would be the Congressmen—not the Presidential Electors—who would decide. Here again, the allies of Martin Van Buren dominated the New York Congressional delegation. The way in which Presidential selection by the House of Representative is specified by the United States Constitution, is that each state, regardless of the number of its congressmen, shall have one vote. The vote of each individual state is determined by a majority vote within the delegation of each state. At the onset of deliberations, the majority of the New York congressional delegation was in favor of Van Buren's choice Crawford. It was New York Congressman, and the Chairmen of the Erie Canal Commission,[43] Steven Van Rensselaer who battled for an endorsement of Adams. In the final tally, Van Rensselaer cast the **tie-breaking** vote within the delegation, that gave the vote of New York to Adams. It was that New York State vote which then **broke the tie** in the House of Representatives and delivered the Presidency to Adams. Without it he would have failed to secure a majority.

FIGURE 5

The Ohio Canal System

Courtesy of the Ohio Department of Natural Resources

The Ties That Bind

• John Jay's son, Peter Augustus Jay, served as the President of the Erie Canal Commission. He also followed in the footsteps of his father as President of the New York Manumission Society, and his single most famous act was a speech he delivered at the New York State Constitutional Convention in 1821, arguing that the right to vote should be extended to free African-Americans. He was also James Fenimore Cooper's closest lifelong friend.

• Steven Van Rensselaer, after leaving Congress in 1829, continued to serve on the Erie Canal Commission until 1839. In 1824, he conceived the idea of establishing a school of higher education "for the purpose of instructing persons, who may choose to apply themselves, in the application of science to the common purposes of life," and he established, entirely with his own funds, the Rensselaer School in Troy, New York (now the Rensselaer Polytechnic Institute), located directly on the route of the Erie Canal. By the 1830s,

---

41. Lincoln's future Secretary of State William Seward also joined the People's Party and campaigned for Clinton. In the 1830s Seward would be active with John Quincy Adams in the Anti-Masonic Party.

42. In 1826 President Adams would appoint the now-elderly King as Ambassador to Great Britain, a position which he had previously held under George Washington.

43. Van Rensselaer succeeded DeWitt Clinton and served as Chairman of the Erie Canal Commission from 1816 to 1830.

Rensselaer's school became the foremost engineering school in United States. Rensselaer's son, Philip, married the daughter of James Tallmadge, the New York Congressman and protégé of DeWitt Clinton who introduced the famous Tallmadge Amendment in 1819 which almost blocked the admission of Missouri as a Slave State.

• Rufus King's son Edward, would marry the daughter of Ohio Governor Worthington, DeWitt Clinton's collaborator in the building of the Ohio-Erie Canal, and then would himself serve as the President of the Erie Canal Commission. Another of his sons, Charles, became president of Columbia College, and Charles' son, Rufus King, Jr., migrated to Wisconsin, was a signer of the Wisconsin State Constitution, a founder of the Wisconsin Republican Party, and an early backer of Abraham Lincoln's Presidential Campaign. In 1863 Lincoln named him Ambassador to the Vatican, and in 1866 King personally arrested the Lincoln assassin John Surratt, who was hiding as a Papal Zouave in Rome!

• James Tallmadge—in addition to his leadership in fighting both the Missouri Compromise and the admission of Arkansas as a Slave Territory, Tallmadge was a fierce advocate of a national economic development policy, including national funding for the Chesapeake and Delaware Canal, (finally built under the Quincy Adams administration). After leaving the Congress, Tallmadge would serve from 1831 to 1850 as the President of the American Institute of the City of New York, an organization devoted to the promotion of inventions and scientific education.

• Peter Cooper—the creator of the Tom Thumb steam locomotive in 1830, the first man to successfully use anthracite coal to puddle iron, and the first person to extensively use the Bessemer blast furnace method, Cooper was a remarkable figure. In the 1830s, he began a years-long collaboration with DeWitt Clinton on the improvement of public education in New York City.[44] This ultimately led to Cooper's decision to create "The Cooper Union for the Advancement of Science and Art," an institution, financed entirely by Cooper, and

___
44. In 1805 DeWitt Clinton had secured a charter for establishing "The Society for Establishing a Free School in the City of New York for the Education of such Poor Children as do not Belong to, or are not Provided for, by any Religious Society." By 1809 a school had been built to house 500 students, and this was greatly expanded over the next 25 years, directed and presided over by Clinton. This was the beginning of the free public school system in New York City.

intended by him to be modeled on the *École Polytechnique* in Paris. Enrollment was free, open to all—men or women, black or white—and aimed primarily at the working class population of the City. In 1860 the Cooper Union hosted the prospective Presidential candidate Abraham Lincoln, and after the attack on Fort Sumter, in April of 1861, a massive public rally was held at Union Square, only nine blocks north of Cooper's school. The 70-year old Cooper was one of the first speakers at the rally, saying:

> We are contending with an enemy not only determined on our destruction as a nation, but to build on our ruins a government devoted with all its power to maintain, extend, and perpetuate a system in itself revolting to all the best feelings of humanity,—an institution that enables thousands to sell their own children into hopeless bondage.
>
> Shall it succeed? You say 'no!' and I unite with you in your decision. We cannot allow it to succeed. We should spend our lives, our property, and leave the land itself a desolation before such an institution should triumph over the free people of this country. ...

In 1864, when there was a strong chance that the Democrat McClellan might carry New York City, it was Cooper who organized a great mass meeting for September 27, 1864, in the Hall of Cooper Union to rally the population behind Lincoln.

In 1876, this Peter Cooper, an enthusiastic supporter of Lincoln's Greenback policy, was nominated and ran as the Presidential candidate of the Greenback Party. Seven years later, when Cooper died at the age of 92, his funeral procession was the largest in the City since that of George Washington.

The Pathfinder & the Candidate

The life and works of James Fenimore Cooper are far too vast a subject for a short work such as this, but let us simply say this:

James Fenimore Cooper's father, William Cooper, was a close political ally to Philip Schuyler, Alexander Hamilton. and John Jay. John Jay's son, Peter Augustus, was James Fenimore's closest and most intimate friend throughout the lives of the two men.

In his young adult years, Cooper formed an intense political loyalty to DeWitt Clinton, which continued until Clinton's death. Later, it would be President John Quincy Adams who would secure Cooper a European Consulship. Essentially, one might say that *the Erie Canal Principle* is to be found in Cooper's personal and political life.

Over a thirty-year period, beginning with the 1821 publication of *The Spy: A Tale of the Neutral Ground* and ending with the 1851 writing of *New York: or The Towns of Manhattan*, Cooper, perhaps more than any other individual, was personally responsible for sustaining and developing the *Idea* of Hamilton's New York. From his attacks on the oligarchy, beginning with *The Bravo*, to his vision of an American Republic

Lincoln at Manhattan's Cooper Union, 1860

of Free (non-slave) Citizens in the *Leatherstocking Tales* and elsewhere, to his chronicling of the civilizing of New York State in the wake of the Erie Canal, it was Cooper who bridged the span from Washington's (Manhattan) inauguration of 1789, to Lincoln's (Manhattan) Cooper Union Speech of 1860.

Cooper's final work, *New York: or The Towns of Manhattan*, remained unfinished and unpublished at the time of his death in 1851, but the completed introduction to that work began to circulate under a variety of titles, including "On Secession and States Rights," shortly after Cooper's death. This work—written ten years before the inauguration of Lincoln—addresses directly the issue of the expansion of slavery into the territories, and the mortal danger that the expansion of the Slave Power poses to the nation. The wording and subject matter of Cooper's final work, echo the battles against the Slave Power going back to the Northwest Ordinance, the Constitutional Convention, and the continuous fight led by Washington's New Yorkers.

Nine years later, Abraham Lincoln delivered his famous Cooper Union Speech at the Great Hall, located at the intersection of Fifth Street and Third Avenue in Manhattan. For those not familiar with the speech, two things should be conveyed. First, this was the singular speech which made possible Lincoln's achievement of

the Republican Party Presidential nomination. Prior to the speech, it was considered almost certain that the nomination would go to New York State's own William Seward. Lincoln came into Seward's home territory and took the hearts and minds of Seward's supporters out from under him.

Second, the subject matter of Lincoln's speech on that occasion, was the mortal danger posed to the Republic by the continuing, rapacious drive by the Slavocracy to expand its power, particularly through the spread of slavery into the territories. In the text of the speech, Lincoln names—name by name— Hamilton, Morris, Jay, and King, as leaders of the Nation who had fought the Slave Power from the beginning.

* * *

Gouverneur Morris once stated that New Yorkers were "born cosmopolite." In a very real way, that short assertion defines the nature of the City. The localism, the backwardness, the rural idiocy of the Southern Slave System, could find no home in New York. Even after the infestation of the financial parasites—Aaron Burr, Martin Van Buren, August Belmont and J.P. Morgan—Manhattan has always been Hamilton's New York, and the financial agents of Empire merely a foreign bacillus that has no legitimate existence. It is still to this day the cultural, educational, financial, and—in a very real sense—the political capital of the United States.

In the mid-1960s, only about two decades after the death of New Yorker Franklin Delano Roosevelt, Lyndon LaRouche initiated a series of classes and lectures at Columbia University —the *alma mater* of Alexander Hamilton, John Jay, and Gouverneur Morris— which attracted young people, and led eventually into the founding of the LaRouche political movement, an association which stands to this day. It is that movement, our movement, which speaks for Hamilton's New York.

Epilogue

On July Ninth, 1804 Gouverneur Morris made the following entry in his diary:

General Hamilton was killed in a duel this morning by Colonel Burr. I go to town, but meet (opposite to the hospital) Martin Wilkins, who tells me General Hamilton is yet alive at Greenwich Street, and not, as I was told this morning, already dead. Go there. When I arrive he is speechless. The scene is too powerful for me, so that I am obliged to walk in the garden to take breath. After having composed myself, I return and sit by his side till he expires. He is opened, and we find that the ball has broken one of his ribs, passed through the lower part of the liver, and lodged in the vertebrae of his back: a most melancholy scene. His wife almost frantic with grief, his children in tears, every person present deeply afflicted, the whole city agitated, every countenance dejected. This evening I am asked to pronounce a funeral oration. I promise to do so if I can possibly command myself enough, but express my belief that it will be utterly impossible. I am wholly unmanned by this day's spectacle.

Two days later, at the request of Elizabeth Hamilton, Morris delivered the Funeral Oration for Alexander Hamilton in Manhattan. These are excerpts:

Fellow-Citizens,

If on this sad, this solemn occasion, I should endeavor to move your commiseration, it would be doing injustice to that sensibility which has been so generally and so justly manifested. Far from attempting to excite your emotions, I must try to repress my own, and yet I fear that instead of the language of a public speaker, you will hear only the lamentations of a bewailing friend. But I will struggle with my bursting heart, to portray that Heroic Spirit, which has flown to the mansions of bliss.

Students of Columbia! He was in the ardent pursuit of knowledge in your academic shades, when the first sound of the American war called him to the field. A young and unprotected volunteer, such was his zeal and so brilliant his service that we heard his name before we knew his person. It seemed as if God had called him suddenly into existence, that he might assist to save a world!

The penetrating eye of Washington soon perceived the manly spirit which animated his youthful bosom. By that excellent judge of men he was selected as an Aide, and thus he became early acquainted with, and was a principal actor in, the most important scenes of our Revolution.

At the siege of York, he pertinaciously insisted and he obtained the command of a Forlorn Hope. He stormed the redoubt; but let it be recorded, that not one single man of the enemy perished. His gallant troops emulating the example of their chief checked the uplifted arm, and spared a foe no longer resisting. Here closed his military career.

Shortly after the war, your favor, no, your discernment called him to public office. You sent him to the convention at Philadelphia: he there assisted in forming that constitution which is now the bond of our union, the shield of our defence and the source of our prosperity. In signing that compact he exprest his apprehension that it did not contain sufficient means of strength for its own preservation; and that in consequence we should share the fate of many other republics and pass through Anarchy to Despotism. We hoped better things. We confided in the good sense of the American people, and above all we trusted in the protecting Providence of the Almighty. On this important subject he never concealed his opinion. He disdained concealment. Knowing the purity of his heart, he bore it as it were in his hand, exposing to every passenger its inmost recesses. This generous indiscretion subjected him to censure from misrepresentation. His speculative opinions were treated as deliberate designs; and yet you all know how strenuous, how unremitting were his efforts to establish and to preserve the constitution. If then his opinion was wrong, pardon, oh! pardon that single error, in a life devoted to your service.

At the time when our government was organized, we were without funds, though not without resources. To call them into action, and establish order in the finances, Washington sought for splendid talents, for extensive information, and above all, he sought for sterling, incorruptible integrity. All these he found in Hamilton... And the result was a rapid advance in power and prosperity, of which there is no example in any other age or nation. The part which Hamilton bore is universally known.

His unsuspecting confidence in professions which he believed to be sincere, led him to trust too much to the undeserving. This exposed him to misrepresentation. He felt himself obliged to resign. The care of a rising family, and the narrowness of his fortune, made it a duty to return to his profession for their support. But though he was compelled to abandon public life, never, no, never for a moment did he abandon the public service. He never lost sight of your interests. I declare to you, before that God in whose presence we are now so especially assembled, that in his most private and confidential conversations, the single objects of discussion and consideration were your freedom and happiness...

Brethren of the Cincinnati! There lies our chief! Let him still be our model. Like him, after a long and faithful public service, let us cheerfully perform the social duties of private life. Oh! he was mild and gentle. In him there was no offence; no guile. His generous hand and heart were open to all....

Fellow Citizens! You have long witnessed his professional conduct, and felt his unrivaled eloquence. You know how well he performed the duties of a citizen. You know that he never courted your favor by adulation, or the sacrifice of his own judgment. You have seen him contending against you, and saving your dearest interests, as it were, in spite of yourselves. And you now feel and enjoy the benefits resulting from the firm energy of his conduct. Bear this testimony to the memory of my departed friend. I charge you to protect his fame. It is all he has left, all that these poor orphan children will inherit from their father. But, my countrymen, that fame may be a rich treasure to you also. Let it be the test by which to examine those who solicit your favour. Disregarding professions, view their conduct and on a doubtful occasion, ask, Would Hamilton have done this thing?

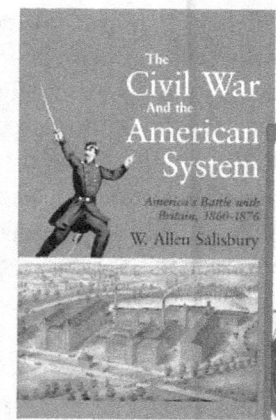
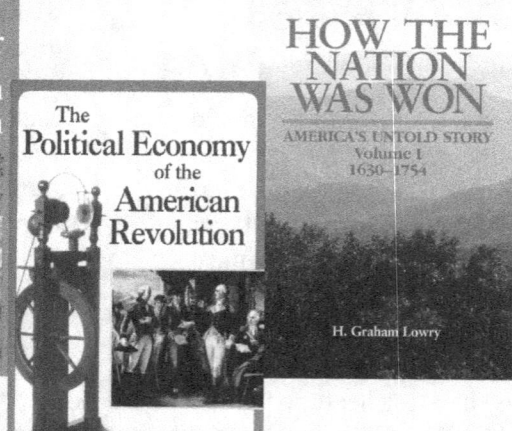

The Baltimore Paradigm: Wall Street's Kill Zones

by Debra Hanania-Freeman

May 4—On May 1, Baltimore's State's Attorney Marilyn Mosby, the city's top prosecutor, announced criminal charges against six Baltimore City police officers in the death of Freddie Gray, the 25-year-old man who suffered a fatal spine injury while in police custody, and whose death sparked rioting and unrest in the city. The charges range from second degree murder, assault, and false imprisonment to lesser charges of misconduct in office.

She gave a preamble before reading the charges:

> To the people of Baltimore and demonstrators across America, I heard your call for no justice, no peace. Your peace is sincerely needed as I work to deliver justice on behalf of this young man. To those that are angry, hurt or have their own experiences of injustice at the hands of police officers, I urge you to channel the energy peacefully as we prosecute this case. To the rank and file officers of the Baltimore City Police Department, please know that these accusations of these six officers are not an indictment on the entire force.

She meant it. Only on the job since January, Mosby, was raised by a single mother whose own mother, father, grandfather, and uncles were all Baltimore police officers.

The announcement brought calm to a city that had suffered six days of rioting, looting, and arson, and was welcomed by local civic, religious, and political leaders, as well as by Mr. Gray's family, as the first step in satisfying the demand of "Justice for Freddie Gray," whose only crime seemed to be making eye contact with a policeman.

However, in order to understand the Gray case, and its aftermath, and in order to even begin to satisfy the demands for "justice," one has to consider just how Baltimore, and cities across the nation, have come to this point. Ultimately, the Gray case isn't about police policy. It is about a battle over the defined mission of the United States and the very conception of man, a battle that has raged since the nation's birth.

Not About Race

For Baltimore to be the setting for the latest in this recent spate of high-profile police-involved deaths makes clear that, while there are undeniably racial issues involved, this is not about race. After all, Baltimore is not Ferguson, Missouri. The city's mayor, chief prosecutor, the majority of the city council, and the police chief are all African-American. More than 50% of Baltimore city police officers are African-American. Indeed, the driver of the van that provided what Baltimoreans refer to as the "nickel ride" (an intentionally rough and violent ride

When Baltimore saved the nation. The militia which stopped the British army cold after it had burned Washington, musters in Patterson Park in central Baltimore in September 1814.

When Baltimore built the nation. At Sparrows Point, the steelmaking process was first integrated from the arrival of tankers with iron ore, to the shipment of finished steel, producing more than 3500 combinations and grades of steel—and enabled most Baltimore families to live on the income of one wage earner.

EPA

in a paddy wagon) that resulted in Gray's severed spine and ultimately, his death, was also black.

But, Baltimore is a city victimized by Wall Street's conscious policy of deindustrialization and globalization unleashed in leading manufacturing cities in America over at least the past 40 years. That policy, now in its end-phase of collapse, has created neighborhoods that are petri dishes for disease, drugs, and crime, often spread through the medium of a very large, revolving prison population, which brings hepatitis, HIV, drug-resistant TB, resurgent syphilis, and high-risk pregnancies out of the prisons and into the general population of extremely impoverished neighborhoods.

Baltimore residents refer to these neighborhoods as "Death Zones."

A Great Labor Force Discarded

It wasn't always this way. From the 1600s, Baltimore, 12 miles inland from the Chesapeake Bay, served as a centrally located port for the original colonies. As the new nation grew, Baltimore grew in importance in manufacturing, commerce, and shipping. It was home to the nation's first railroad, with key rail links to the west, north, and south.

During those early days, the battle also raged between what Robert Ingraham identifies as the New York leadership that created the U.S. Constitution and defined the nation's mission under George Washington's Presi-

dency, and the anti-human Slavocracy of the South (see p. 4). The War of 1812's famous Battle of Baltimore in 1814 saw local citizens manning the guns of Fort McHenry, and ultimately forcing the retreat and humiliating defeat of Britain's mighty naval armada. It was, of course, during that battle that Francis Scott Key penned what was later to become the National Anthem.

Less than 50 years later, the Slavocracy had entrenched itself in the city to such an extent that, by 1861, the guns of Fort McHenry were turned against the city, to guarantee that the train carrying President Lincoln to his inauguration be allowed safe passage.

Following the Civil War, the American System once again prevailed. In 1887, the Pennsylvania Steel Company brought the steel process to a facility on Baltimore's southeast tip known as Sparrows Point. There, in an advance over British steel production, the steelmaking process was integrated in a single facility, from the arrival of tankers with iron ore, to the shipment of finished steel, eventually producing more than 3,500 combinations and grades of steel. During World War II, the Sparrows Point plant (then owned by Bethlehem Steel) produced more than 17 million tons of steel.

During FDR's transformation of the U.S. economy into the "Arsenal of Democracy" for World War II, Baltimore employed 260,000 workers in manufacturing activity. Three shipyards employed 77,000 workers; the aircraft industry, which included a converted GM assembly plant, employed 50,000, and the Sparrows Point integrated steel complex employed 29,000.

The city became a magnet for workers. Thousands of African-Americans from all over the rural South travelled to Baltimore for high-paying manufacturing jobs, joining Germans, Poles, Irish, Italians, and others migrating south from Pennsylvania coal country. Wages were high enough for all these workers to purchase homes and raise their families on the income of one person. The cultural outlook was one of production and was prevalent throughout the school and college systems, with training in metallurgy and other kinds of science and technology. Post-war, the steel and general manufacturing base of the Baltimore metropolitan area continued to thrive.

The Death Spiral

And then, it all changed.

The deindustrialization of Baltimore began in the 1970s with the shrinkage of steel, shipbuilding, auto, and other industrial producers, and a city that had been a center of innovation and industry since the American Revolution, was progressively turned into a decayed shell, whose population is living out a 21st-Century death spiral.

Over the last 40 years, Baltimore has been taken apart and reassembled, with no high-paying manufacturing industry and a loss of over one-third of its population. Among those who have jobs, 90% work in service industries related to tourism and the Johns Hopkins Medical complex, which is now the city's largest employer. Much of the population lives in what are essentially slave quarters, servicing entertainment complexes as ticket takers, food service workers, and janitors. According to the last census, about 30% of the city's households are headed by single mothers who live in poor, segregated neighborhoods created by deindustrialization, in which a majority of the adults are either unemployed or have dropped out of, or never been a part of, the labor force.

Baltimore's black population has undoubtedly suffered the worst of it. Last year, the *Baltimore Sun* documented a litany of police abuse of black people as routine as it was savage, with compensation payouts of $5.7 million since 2011 for the few cases pursued and vindicated. This, in the city where Wells Fargo paid millions to settle a lawsuit claiming it steered black homeowners, in particular, into subprime mortgages they could not afford.

In Sandtown-Winchester, the West Baltimore neighborhood where Freddie Gray grew up and was chased by the police, life expectancy is 69.7 years, on par with Iraq and Kazakhstan. According to the 2010 census, more than half the households had incomes less than

FIGURE 1

Baltimore 'Death Zones'—Areas (Circled) of High Disease, Poverty, and Death Rates, Inside the City Borders

(Base Map Shows Percentages of Households with Annual Incomes Under $30,000, by Census Tract, 2000)

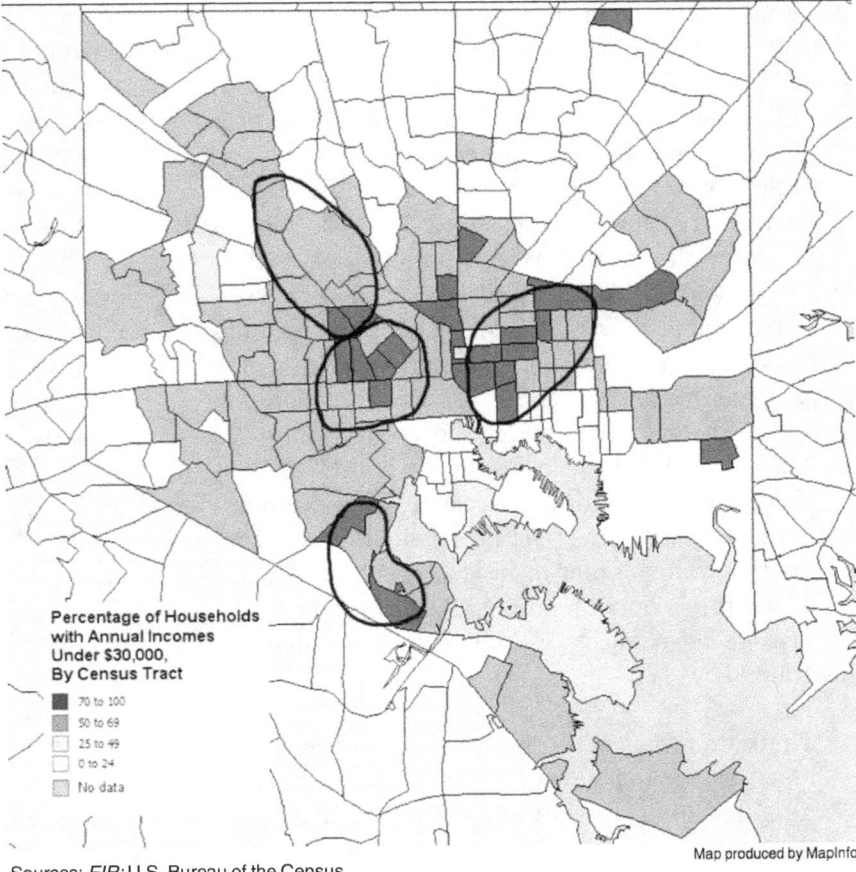

Sources: *EIR*; U.S. Bureau of the Census.

When Wall Street destroyed Baltimore. It's not race: With employment shipped south and abroad under "free trade," Sparrows Point shut down, the high rates of unemployment, incarceration, and health problems have created "death zones."

$25,000. Unemployment was double the city average (already one of the highest unemployment rates in the nation). A more recent study found that Sandtown-Winchester had the highest rate in the city of residents who were incarcerated. Long before Freddie Gray was treated to the nickel ride that led to his death, he and his twin sister were plaintiffs in a lawsuit against the city because they suffered lead-paint poisoning in substandard city housing.

But the shocking reality is that Sandtown is typical of the neighborhoods—or more appropriately, the Killing Zones—across a city where less than 50% of those who make it to high school actually graduate. Still more shocking is the fact that the same pattern prevails nationwide.

Why Has It Happened?

Thirty-five years ago, the U.S. ranked 13th among the 34 industrialized nations that are today in the OECD, in terms of life expectancy for newborns. Today it ranks 29th. In 1980, the infant mortality rate in the U.S. was the same as in Germany. Today, American babies die at twice the rate of German babies. A report by the National Research Council and the Institute of Medicine says, "On nearly all indicators of mortality, survival and life expectancy, the United States ranks at or near the bottom among high-income countries."

If there is anything positive to come of the tragedy of Freddie Gray, it is that it has forced at least some of America's political leaders to confront this reality. Many would prefer to just talk about racism or, as Hillary Clinton did, judicial reform. And both issues deserve discussion. More importantly, though, is that the tragedy has moved the discussion of the underlying causes of what happened in Baltimore to the fore.

Martin O'Malley, who served as both Mayor of Baltimore and Governor of Maryland before considering a run for the Democratic presidential nomination, cut short a speaking tour of Ireland to return to Baltimore when the riots broke out. Before taking to the streets to talk to residents, O'Malley issued a statement, insisting:

> The burning anger in the heart of our city—broadcast around the world—reminded all of us of a hard truth. It is a truth we must face as a nation. Because it is a truth that threatens our children's future. It is the reality that eats away at the heart of America and the very survival of the American Dream we share.
>
> The hard, truthful reality is this: growing numbers of our fellow citizens in American cities across the United States feel unheard, unseen, unrecognized—their very lives unneeded.
>
> This is not just about policing in America. This is about everything it is supposed to mean to be an American.
>
> As Dr. Martin Luther King once said, 'a riot is the language of the unheard.' And, this week the people of our city and our entire country were forced to listen.
>
> Listen to the anger of young American men who are growing into adulthood with grim prospects of survival and even lesser prospects of success.
>
> Listen to the fears of young men with little hope of a finding a summer job, let alone, a job that might one day support a family.
>
> Listen to the silent scream within the vacant hearts of young American boys who feel that America has forgotten them, that America doesn't care about them, that America wishes not to look at them, that America wishes they would go away or be locked away.
>
> Make no mistake about it, the anger that we have seen in Ferguson, in Cleveland, in Staten Island, in North Charleston, and in the flames of Baltimore is not just about policing.
>
> It is about the legacy of race that would have us devalue black lives—whether their death is caused by a police officer or at the hand of another young black man.
>
> It is about declining wages and the lack of opportunity in our country today.
>
> It is about the brutality of an economic system that devalues human labor, human potential, and human lives.
>
> It is about the lie that we make of the American Dream when we put the needs of the most powerful wealthy few ahead of the well-being of our nation's many.
>
> Extreme poverty is extremely dangerous.
>
> This is not just about policing. Not just about race.

In a May 3 appearance on NBC's Meet the Press, O'Malley, who has made the restoration of Glass-Steagall the cornerstone of his campaign, added, "Look at the structure that we have in our economy, the way we ship jobs and profits abroad, the way we fail to invest in our infrastructure and fail to invest in American cities. We are creating these conditions. Surely we are capable of more as a nation."

Needed: A New Presidency

But even O'Malley, who clearly recognizes the problem, has yet to lay out a detailed solution for the nation as a whole, despite the fact that the solution is readily available.

American economist and statesman Lyndon LaRouche has emphasized that that solution will require assembling a "Presidential team," of which O'Malley's Glass-Steagall commitment is just one aspect; Sen. Elizabeth Warren's war on Wall Street is another. More than simply naming poverty and past deindustrialization is necessary. For example, there is the crucial issue of water—creating water for the West, stricken by a drought which could do to our nation's most productive regions, what Wall Street did to Baltimore.

Instead, Baltimore could revive by again helping build the infrastructure to bring water to the West.

But this requires action guided by scientific principles and technological discoveries; LaRouche's Science Team has laid them out for that next "Presidential team."

Even George Washington, in the Presidency, was not enough: Without Treasury Secretary Alexander Hamilton's credit policy and Hamilton's New York team, the nation's historically unprecedented economic growth and strength would not have been launched from 1790 on.

President Obama will have to be forced from office to stop the destruction of his and Bush's endless wars. And that Presidential team will have to take the United States into the new world economic order being fashioned by the BRICS nations and new institutions like the Asian Infrastructure Investment Bank (AIIB).

If we do that, then, and only then, can we be satisfied that we have won some justice for all the Freddie Grays of these United States.

When America Started Downhill

In April 1968, Robert F. Kennedy was on a plane heading for a campaign rally in Indianapolis when he was told that Martin Luther King was shot dead. He was told to call off the rally. The chief of police warned him not to go into the ghetto. His police escort abandoned him as he entered the ghetto. The crowd that gathered had not heard the news of King's death. Kennedy told them. He ended:

> Let us dedicate ourselves to what the Greeks wrote so many years ago: To tame the savageness of man and make gentle the life of the world. Let us dedicate ourselves to that.

Over the next days there were riots in 110 cities. Thirty-nine people were killed, mostly black. There were 75,000 troops in the street. There were no riots in Indianapolis where Kennedy was campaigning. He went to Cleveland and said,

> Violence goes on and on. Why? What has violence accomplished? What has it ever created? No martyr's cause has ever been stilled by his assassin's bullet.

RFK's biographer writes:

> He flew back to Washington, a city of smoke and flame, under curfew, patrolled by trooops.

He walked through the Black districts. Burning wood and broken glass were all over the place. Walter Fauntroy said, "The troops were on duty. A crowed followed behind us, following Bobby Kennedy. The troops saw us coming at a distance, and they put on gas masks and got their guns at ready, waiting for this horde of Blacks coming up the street. When they saw it was Bobby Kennedy, they took off their gas masks and let us through. They looked awfully relieved."

During the worst of the urban riots of 1967 Kennedy, though advised not to, toured the Black and Hispanic areas. When asked what he would do if he became President, Kennedy said he would make the media show what it was like to live in the ghettos. He said:

> Let them show the soul, the feel, the hopelessness, and what it's like to think, you'll never get out. Show a Black teenager, told by some radio jingle to stay in school, looking at his older brother who stayed in school and is out of a job. Show the Mafia pushing narcotics; put a candid camera team in a ghetto school and watch what a rotten system of education it really is.... Ask people to watch it—and experience what it was like to live the most affluent society in history—without hope.

On June 6, 1968, RFK won the California primary and was heading for the Presidency. That day he was shot dead.

—Donald Phau

What Is the Future Of Mankind?

by Matthew Ogden

Good evening; it's May 1, 2015. My name is Matthew Ogden, and I will be hosting tonight's webcast here from larouchepac.com. I'm joined in the studio tonight by Benjamin Deniston and Megan Beets, both from the LaRouchePAC Scientific Research Team, who will be presenting an up-to-date report on ongoing work that they and their team have been continuing to develop.

As Mr. LaRouche specified during a meeting we had with him this morning, the theme of tonight's webcast is "<u>What Is the Future of Mankind?</u>"

The topics which you will hear tonight will be ideas which will challenge you, and will challenge what you think you know about the world around you. They might not be ideas that are necessarily popular, or which you are personally familiar with as of yet; but after going through tonight's proceedings, you will hopefully gain an apprehension, at least, of a universe beyond what you thought you knew before, and a reality beyond what you have previously accepted as self-evident experience. And in so doing, we intend to create in your imagination an image of the potential available to us to create, if we adopt those necessary actions.

And from that standpoint, I'd like to emphasize that what Megan and Ben will present tonight, is by no means a subject matter abstracted from the great dangers facing mankind at the present time. But rather, they must be understood as an integral part of the great political and historical drama in which the world is now engaged. It must be seen from the standpoint of living history, a living history in which we—all of us—are actors; actively and willfully creating the future and the form of the options which are available to mankind. New principles, new modes of action, which will dramatically change mankind's view of himself as a species.

Crises from California to the Middle East

Now, just look for a moment, before we get to that, at the crisis that is now confronting us. Look out and survey the utter devastation which we now face both in Europe and here in the United States: the drought in California, the riots in Baltimore, the drownings in the Mediterranean, the spreading war and terrorism across the Middle East, the rise of fascism on the borders of Russia—sponsored by Obama and Victoria Nuland—and the looming threat of thermonuclear war. The conclusion cannot be made more clear: we cannot continue to operate within the paradigm of this dying system.

What has been accepted heretofore as tradition and popular opinion has absolutely failed; and only a handful of leaders, who have the courage to overturn those traditions, and to confront the failings and the falsehoods of popularly accepted opinion, will be successful in creating the future.

Civilization, especially in this part of the planet, can only survive if we can succeed in creating an entirely new paradigm, by choosing an alternative system which is now coming into being in China and the other nations associated with the BRICS—as Helga Zepp-LaRouche very clearly and beautifully presented in a short video,

USDA/David Kosling

The drought in California has caused this riverbed in Bakersfield, along Highway 99, to dry up (Feb. 26, 2014).

which was posted on this website this week. It is called "A New Paradigm for Civilization,"and is a video which I strongly encourage you to watch and to share as widely as you can.

Now, as many people know, V-E Day is a week from today—May 8—on which day we celebrate the 70th anniversary of the defeat of fascism in Europe during World War II. In Russia, this is observed on May 9. Our allies in that war—especially Russia and China—were critical in securing the victory alongside President Franklin Roosevelt, who was the greatest U.S. President of the 20th Century. This was a war in which 27 million Russians died—which was 13% of the entire population of the Soviet Union at that time, as well as approximately 20 million Chinese, according to certain estimates.

And the effect of this war remains vividly imprinted in the living memories of those alive today, whose fathers and brothers, and sometimes even sisters and mothers, fought and died in that war.

President Putin himself is counted among those. President Putin just published a very rare editorial piece in which he remembered his brother—who perished during the siege of Leningrad—and his father, who was nearly killed by a German grenade.

So you can imagine the utter horror of the people of these nations, which these nations feel when they see a resurgence of fascism in places like Ukraine: a fascism which is being actively supported and encouraged by Obama and members of his administration, who have subverted and usurped the office of the once-great institution of the Presidency of the United States, the same office which Presidents Franklin Roosevelt, Abraham Lincoln, and George Washington once held.

Recreating the Institution of the Presidency

Now, as we've elaborated on previous broadcasts here, the intent of LaRouchePAC at this time is to recreate the institution of the American Presidency, in the image of what its founders intended it to be.

I'd like to draw our viewers' attention in that regard, to an article which will be published soon in *Executive Intelligence Review* magazine, by Bob Ingraham, who is an historian and an active member of the LaRouche movement out in California. In this article he vividly elaborates the mortal struggle of Alexander Hamilton and his circle of allies in New York State, against the traitors from among the Southern slaveholders and their allies on Wall Street, who began their attempts to destroy the constitutional republic which Alexander Hamilton and Washington had created, from the very first day of Washington's Presidency, if not before, and which they continue to do to this day; those efforts have not ceased.

As Mr. LaRouche has repeatedly pointed out, only rarely have we had truly great Presidents who stand in the tradition of Washington and Hamilton, assume the office of the President of the United States. And it's only been through the efforts of those few, that this nation has even survived to the present.

The Potential O'Malley Candidacy

Now earlier today, we discussed with Mr. LaRouche an institutional question which came in for him this morning. The question was simple and to the point, and I think germane to this subject. It reads, very briefly, as

White House/Pete Souza

Obama, said Lyndon LaRouche, is becoming even more rapacious as his Presidency disintegrates.

follows: "Mr. LaRouche, in your view, should Martin O'Malley announce his candidacy for the Democratic nomination for President?"

Mr. LaRouche's response was that it was not necessarily his place to involve himself in the details, and tell O'Malley specifically what he should do and when he should do it. But, that if you look at the process that is now underway, O'Malley's candidacy is extremely significant and unique; especially when you view his rise as counterposed to the accelerating rate of decline of Hillary Clinton's candidacy.

Mr. LaRouche said, with her failure to be a credible candidate at this point, O'Malley comes up as presently the only viable and credible contender to the Bushes and to the Republican Party. And then, if you factor in to this the accelerating decline of Obama, with the trap which he is essentially setting up for himself with the TPP, where he's openly attacking leading members of his own party such as Elizabeth Warren, Sherrod Brown, and others, then it's clear that Obama can be taken down, and a very credible team can be put together around an O'Malley candidacy—which is now beginning to take shape.

And I should mention that the so-called "Manhattan Project"—this initiative in New York City which Mr. LaRouche launched in the fall of last year—is playing a very significant role in this process. That can be seen both by the introduction of a Glass-Steagall resolution in the New York State Assembly, which is gaining broad support, as well as the passage of an anti-TPP resolution in the New York City Council, which we just received news of today.

This resolution declares the City of New York to be a "TPP-free zone" and urges Congress to oppose President Obama's attempts to obtain so-called "fast track" authority to negotiate and approve the TPP with only the 'yea' or 'nay' of Congress. So this is clearly a major challenge to Obama, coming from the heart of New York City, and represents a very significant revolt from within the Democratic Party.

Now the point that Mr. LaRouche made this afternoon, was that Obama was clearly crumbling, but he's not his own man. Obama represents his masters; and their effort will be to try to use him as an instrument to launch a world war, even as he's collapsing. He is increasingly losing his power, but as a result of this, his predisposition towards rage will incline him toward launching just such a world war while he still has hold of his Presidency.

And Mr. LaRouche said that Obama, in his decline, is becoming even more rapacious, and even more murderous, and even more of a killer, because of his rage at his own decline. And therefore, in light of the increasingly obvious failure as of now, of the Hillary Clinton candidacy, the most significant factor at this point, is the campaign being run by O'Malley and the O'Malley/Warren team, you could call it, who are clearly on the rise.

'A Riot—the Language of the Unheard'

And for those who saw it, I think Martin O'Malley's statements on the riots in Baltimore were absolutely to the point on this. And I'd just like to read a short excerpt from them. I think if people heard Mr. LaRouche's comments on this subject during our discussion with the members of the LaRouchePAC Policy Committee on Monday, only a few hours before the violence broke out in Baltimore, what O'Malley had to say on this I think will resonate. O'Malley's statement reads as follows:

"As Dr. Martin Luther King once said, 'a riot is the language of the unheard.' This week, the people of our city and our entire country, were forced to listen; to listen to the anger of young American men who are growing into adulthood with grim prospects of survival, and even lesser prospects of success. To listen to the fears of young men with little hope of finding a summer job, let alone a job that might one day support a family. To listen to the silent scream within the vacant hearts of young American boys, who feel that America has forgotten them; that America doesn't care about them. That America wishes not to look at them; that America wishes they would go away, or be locked away. Surely, we are capable of more as a nation."

O'Malley continued: But the anger that we have seen in Ferguson, in Cleveland, in Staten Island, in North Charleston, and in the flames of north Baltimore, is not just about policing; it is not just about race.

"It is about declining wages and the lack of opportunity in our country today. It is about the brutality of an economic system that devalues human labor, human potential, and human lives. It is about the lie that we make of the American dream, when we put the needs of the most powerful wealthy ahead of the well-being of our nation's many. Extreme poverty is extremely dangerous. This is about the country we are allowing ourselves to become, and the affront that it is to the country that we are meant to be. We are Americans, and we are still capable of remaking our future. And this generation of Americans still has time to be called great. But only our actions can save us."

So, I think this is actually very appropriate to the theme of tonight's webcast. What is the future of our nation? What is the future of mankind? And when everything is collapsing, when civilization is crumbling, when Europe and the United States are disintegrating and the lives of our people are getting worse and worse at an accelerating rate, what is the solution? How do we create the future?

And the future is always defined not by what you already know, not by what you already experienced; but rather by what you don't know, by what mankind has never before experienced. So with that said, I'd like to hand the podium over to Megan Beets, who will deliver a short introduction to this evening's presentation by Ben.

As Kepler Shows Us, Man Is Not an Animal

by Megan Beets

Thank you, Matthew. Now as Matt just said, the mission at hand, the mission which all of us here in the LaRouche movement have taken up, and the mission which we pose to all of you, is to create a future for civilization. One of the most important people who will determine whether or not that effort to create a future for civilization will succeed or fail, is the figure of Johannes Kepler, who died in 1630.

So why is Kepler one of the most crucial human beings present—in a certain way—in society today? Kepler proved in practice, through his discovery of the Solar System, that mankind is not a species of animal. Now, Kepler lived 400 years ago, and he lived at a time in Europe which was engulfed in the flames of religious war for generations, and in the midst of a dark age—not unlike what stares us in the face today.

However, Kepler's legacy draws not from what he was surrounded by in his daily life, but Kepler goes straight to the Italian Renaissance and to the great mind of Cardinal Nicholas of Cusa, who was the founder of modern scientific method.

Concepts Beyond Sense Perception

Now Cusa posited the idea that man, being an image of the Creator, has a mind which can generate conceptions which are completely beyond and above the imaging power of sense perception, concepts which have no existence in the realm of sense perception, and yet, are true hypotheses about the mind of God.

Now Kepler followed his teacher Cusa. And Kepler proved with his scientific work that man indeed has a mental life; has mental processes which are not derivatives of the information gathered via sense perception and observations; that man has a mental experience that goes beyond the furthest reach of sense perception. And this mental experience is the source of concepts about principles shaping the universe which are true.

Now that is the essence of science. Kepler presents this in detail very clearly, in one of his last works, called the *Harmony of the World*. In that work Kepler begins from the knowledge of the nature of the motion of the planets which is based on a revolutionary conception that he had proven ten years earlier: that the Sun was a physical force; the Sun was not just a passive observer of the motions of the Solar System, as had been believed by all of his predecessors. But the Sun itself is the seat of the physical power which causes the motions of the planets; and the Sun itself is a changing physical process.

Now based upon that, Kepler was able to ask the question: what is the unifying principle of the Solar System as a One? What is the single principle which unites the multiplicity of motions of the entire system as the unfolding of one single intention?

Another way to say the same thing is: why are all of

Frankfurt University

Johannes Kepler

the motions of the Solar System as they are, and not otherwise?

Now, Kepler discovered that each of the planets' motions is not an individual motion. No planet is acting as an individual being, but each planet's motion belongs to a set of tuned motions, much like the individual member of a string quartet isn't acting on his own, but is responding and participating in the unfolding of one unified, tuned whole.

A Single Tuned Unity

Now. Kepler discovered this, not by calculation, not by mathematics, but by generating within his mind an original idea—as if he had created the Solar System from the start—of what the principle of the composition of the Solar System ought to be. So he conceived of the physical power of the Sun, serving the function of tuning and regulating each motion within it, to reflect a single tuned unity, which reflected a system of human polyphonic music.

So, in other words, Kepler re-cast the Solar System as an object of human thought, as a human system. And he was right. And because of Kepler, for the first time, man's mind encompassed the principle of the Solar System.

Now, animals don't do this. Animals are bound to earth. Animals are creatures of their senses. They respond to stimuli, they adjust their behavior based on stimuli, they adjust their behavior to adapt to the circumstances of the environment around them. But man is different. Man in his essence is a creature of a higher power.

So Kepler has left us with this legacy. He took the first step of discovery of the Solar System, but as I think Ben will open up for us, what we know today is that the earth and the Solar System are encompassed, subsumed, within an even larger system. We know that the earth itself is part of this larger galactic system which has effects directly for everyone living on earth. And so the challenge and the mission before *us*, which I'm going to ask Ben to come to the podium to elaborate, is how do we begin to tackle that—mastering that principle of the galactic system and the legacy of Kepler.

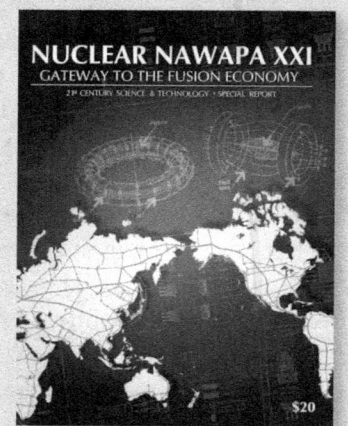

Creating the Future

by Benjamin Deniston

Thanks, Megan.

Some of this comes directly out of our discussion with Mr. LaRouche earlier today, and his emphasis on including this as a featured part of our intervention in this point of the discussion. And I think, as you just posed it very clearly, it needs to be clear to people that Kepler provides a reference point for the creation of the future, for where we need to go, as much as what he did to define this revolution of the past, so to speak.

And this does not mean that he gives us some practical solutions or something. The average person will say: Okay, does he tell us, where to get the water now? or something silly like that. He doesn't give us a playbook that you can go run to. He gives us something more important than that. He gives us an understanding of how mankind is able to develop new solutions to new problems—a better understanding of, as Megan was discussing, how it is that mankind uniquely relates to the universe, and how mankind can change that relation. You know, these are the big questions that we are facing right now as a species.

In that context, an expression of that, we have this water crisis. We have a major crisis developing in California immediately; other locations in the Southwest are maybe one or two steps behind California. Other places around the world are also facing similar water crises. So let's take this in this context.

The water crisis in California—first of all, there are clear levels to the crisis, it's not just one thing. On the first level, we have a drought. We have an immediate drought right now. It hasn't rained much; there hasn't been a lot of precipitation for the past years. So the amount of water coming into the state is lower. That's one aspect, but that's not the entire picture.

You go to a deeper level: there's been no development in the state for water projects, these types of things, for nearly 50 years. For nearly 50 years, there's been no major investment in developing the water resources that we knew were needed. Desalination was put on the table—it wasn't done. NAWAPA was put on the table—it wasn't done. And so, for the past, almost 50 years, we haven't even been operating at break-even; we've been actually drawing down the system in California. We've been consistently depleting the aquifers in the Central Valley, for example, for decades.

This current drought is not a new, out-of-the-blue thing. We've known we've been operating beyond the capacity of the water system of the state as it existed, for decades now. We refused to take action. And now we have a drought hitting on top of that, so that's creating a certain culmination in the crisis.

Brown versus Humanity

But there's another level, there's another aspect on the water crisis in California right now, which is the response of the governor. He is another layer to the crisis.

Governor Brown himself is a crisis in California. You have the drought, and you have the Brown crisis— that's an additional aspect. His response is to say, we're just going to impose a policy of—essentially, population reduction. Whether he is fully recognizing this or not, he is completely buying into the policy of the British Empire, the policy of Prince Philip, the World Wildlife Fund. He is fully on board with that entire program: genocide, population reduction. That's the policy response that he is putting on the table in reaction to this current crisis in California.

So, how do we handle this crisis now? What do we actually do, to address the imminent water crisis in California? Well, the first thing is obvious, we've said it, we're going to continue to say it: Get rid of Jerry Brown. The first step is, you take out the trash; get rid of the problem, get rid of the active factor worsening the situation, now, which is Jerry Brown.

But, that aside, that done, as we want to really elaborate here today, we also need the positive solutions. We need to act human, we need to act creatively. We need to create new solutions, create, in effect, a new future condition which doesn't yet exist. Something which Jerry Brown either doesn't understand, or he doesn't want. But either way, he is right now acting to suppress the people of California, to deny them their natural human right for creative progress. He is acting as a modern lackey of Zeus. That is what he is doing.

So the only true *real* solutions, aside from taking out the garbage—getting rid of Jerry Brown, getting rid of his policy—as Megan introduced this aspect of the discussion here, are for mankind to create the new conditions which don't yet exist. The action of the creation of new states, new conditions in the universe, which would never have existed without mankind's creation, without mankind's intervention. And the creation of these new conditions, new states, which are new to mankind himself—that's where the solution lies.

And that's what we want to discuss.

Mankind discovers things. We discover principles, we discover insights into how the universe operates. But I would say that the clearest, the most pure expression of this process, is that by that activity, we are enabled to change our behavior as a result of these discoveries of principle. We are enabled to do things which we simply couldn't do before.

So again, this is mankind: By his fundamental nature, mankind is a creative species *in this respect*. It's always doing something new, always going to a higher level. We're uniquely a species which continues to change how it relates to the universe. We're not defined by any particular relationship to the universe. We don't have an ecology; the way animals have an ecology. Human ecology is the potential to change our ecology, that's what makes us different from animals, that's what makes us human. So to deny that, to suppress that, as Brown is doing, as Obama is doing in a different sense, but in the same way, really, is true Zeus. It's a Zeusian genocide program. So that's the challenge we face right now in California.

But again, where do we find the solutions, true human solutions to this water crisis? How do we develop new ways to manage the water system, to deal with the water cycle, using methods which might not even exist yet, or haven't existed yet, or, if they exist, they only exist in very preliminary phases. How can we come to a new, higher level management of the system that we've never been able to develop before? Because if we're not doing that, we're not being human; we're not responding to the crisis as a real

gov.ca.gov

California Gov. Jerry Brown (right) is fully on board with the British Imperial policy of population reduction, genocide.

human species. We're just reacting, the way we did in the past.

So this is the issue, the issue that Mr. LaRouche has put on the table, or emphasized regarding this issue for a couple of years now, actually, when discussing the water crisis, discussing the situation. He was saying, forget just these off-the-shelf, old ideas; we're in an accelerated crisis, we've got to go to higher levels. Where are the higher levels? Where are the subsuming principles? What are the areas we don't yet fully understand, we haven't yet grasped, we don't yet fully understand?

Kepler's Principle

And this takes us to the galaxy, to the galactic system, and it takes us to Kepler for how to think about that, how to approach that. So you can ask, how did Kepler discover the Solar System? What's the importance of referencing Kepler's work here?

Kepler asked how the planets moved, he asked why did the planets move. But what he showed was that nothing in domain of sense-perception could ever account for the planetary motions. He was not the first; as others had done before, Kepler recorded the motions, and he also used other people's recordings of the motions. He could catalogue the effects. A map can be developed, charting the motions of the planets, charting how they move through the sky.

But the map does not tell you how or why the planets actually move, why they move as they do. You're cataloguing an expression, you're mapping a shadow. The effect can be seen, it can be recorded, it can be mapped, it can be charted, but the *cause* of that effect, the source of that shadow, can never be understood in these terms. That's what Kepler showed us. And he showed, and he even discussed very explicitly, as Megan referred to in his last work, his *Harmony of the World*: In there is a brilliant exposition on not just the laws of planetary motion, but the laws of how human mind comes to understand principles.

He doesn't just talk about some formula that tells you how the planets move. He goes through a whole exhaustive development of how it is that the human mind can even come to know that, from his own standpoint, as somebody who you should put some weight behind his idea—because he did it. So he was expressing his own insights, referring to Cusa's work, referring to this method of thought, how he was able to come to his discoveries.

And he says very explicitly and clearly, it's an action of the human mind which enables mankind to understand causes. It didn't come from experience, it didn't come from data from observation. It was a creative action that he generated in his mind. Something he uniquely made which wasn't derived from the evidence. It was something he had to generate, unique and anew, and in certain cases, explicitly, because the evidence he was presented with otherwise, was contradictory. It was inconsistent; it couldn't work itself in its own terms. So he was forced to come up with new conceptions, a new conception that he generated which couldn't have come from anywhere but his own action, his own creative discovery.

So this is a lesson for how we think about, how we relate to the system as a whole. As a human being with a healthy human mind, you observe things, you observe phenomena. You recognize these phenomena as effects; you hypothesize what governs these witnessed effects, and ultimately the demonstration of the validity of your hypotheses, is, whether they enable you, if they enable mankind to change how he operates in the universe. Do your hypotheses allow mankind to do new things? To create new actions? In Mr. LaRouche's work on economics, you can measure this in a certain sense even more clearly: Do they enable an increase in the potential relative population density of the human species? Do they enable a measurable increase in the power of

mankind to expand its influence on the planet and beyond?

In this context, where do we find these types of truly human solutions to this current water crisis—the crisis in California, the crisis in the Southwest? It is by going to these higher levels.

Now it's never complete and final knowledge. You never have a complete, final solution to the entire system. You develop these hypotheses; you demonstrate their validity by showing they give mankind an ability to be more effective, develop a greater power to act in the universe. But sometimes, we witness effects which we could say, violate our existing hypotheses. We see effects, we see phenomena which operate in a way our current hypotheses, our current conceptions, can't account for. And these are great. These inconsistencies—that's what we want. These are our ticket to the future.

These are indications not that we failed—oh, we don't get everything—these are indications that there's a new principle at play. There's a new factor in there that we didn't understand yet, expressing itself, in what we might call an unexpected deviation, an unexpected variation in the shadows, in how the shadows behave. We had some conception of what was casting those shadows, and we see they behave a little bit differently than we would have expected. That's what we want. Those are the types of things that we need to look for, in these types of issues.

The Water Cycle: A Shadow of the Galaxy

Then this brings us back to the water crisis, the theme here: How do we deal with water? How do we deal with the water situation in California? Again, you're dealing with a phenomenon, you're dealing with certain phenomena. We experienced aspects of this thing we objectify, we call as a "water cycle." We see the processes of the motion of water from one location to another; we see the transition of water from one state to another state, from liquid to gas, to ice, to solid, moving through these different states. We see water moving through different processes, through abiotic systems, through biological systems, through human economic activity. So you see all these effects, these phenomena, but no one thinks that the water cycle is a self-determined thing—maybe you find some people who do, but people don't think that this is some self-defined, self-determined process.

It's not hard to recognize, when you identify this thing you call a water cycle, that you're looking at the

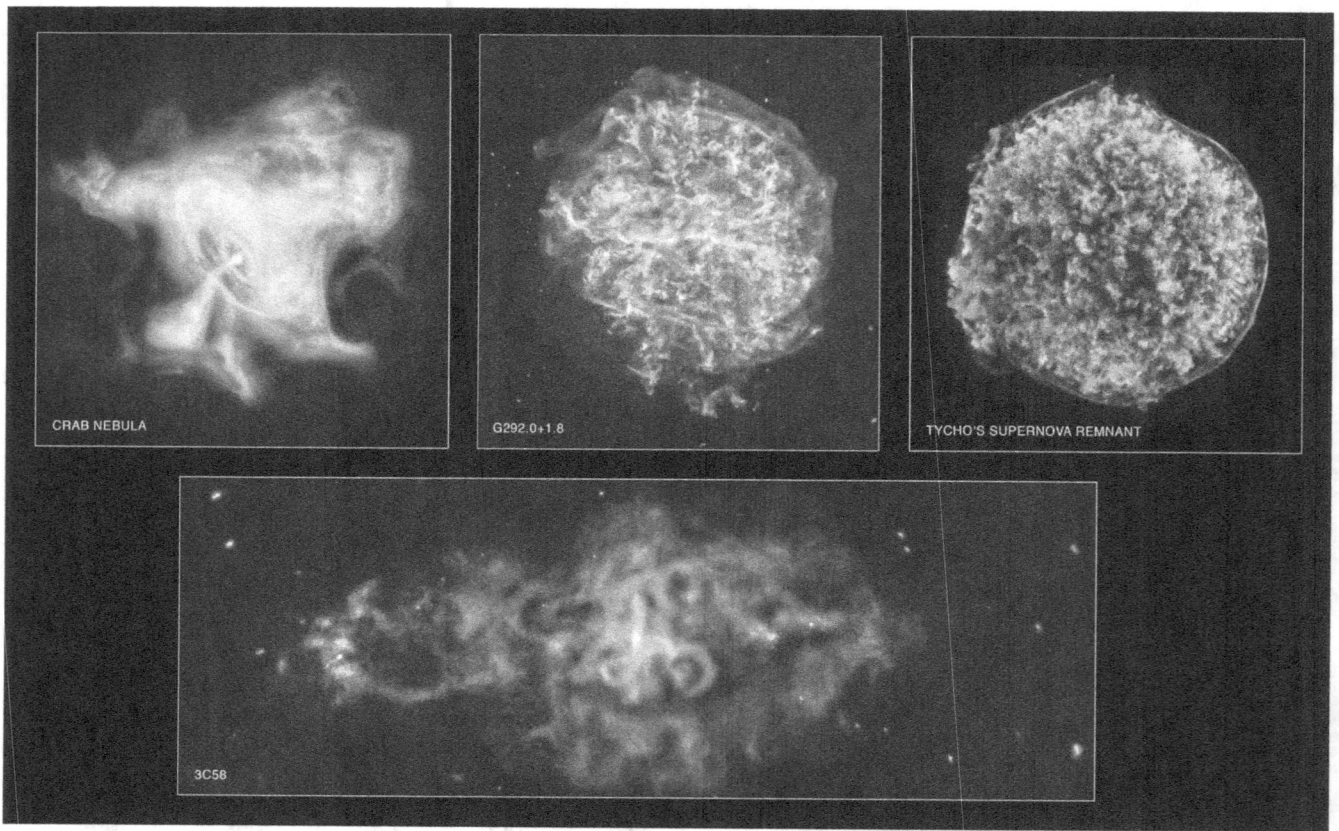

The source of the galactic cosmic radiation permeating the galaxy is thought to be the supernovae of stars. Here four images of supernova remnants illustrate the process some scientists think produces cosmic rays.

expression of certain principles acting, certain forces at play: the role of the Sun. The water cycle wouldn't exist if the Sun didn't exist. The heat effect from the Sun, the electromagnetic radiation from the Sun powers the whole cycle; it evaporates ocean water, it gets the sky filled with atmospheric moisture. The rotation of the Earth is a critical factor in determining how the system behaves, the motion of atmospheric water through the sky, related to the wind patterns and effects associated with the rotation of the Earth.

You have the action of life: Plant life, in particular, plays a major role in putting water back up into the atmosphere. Water that's on land that would have just remained on land— plant life is pumping it back up.

No one thinks the water cycle is some self-defined, existing thing; we already know it as a shadow. We know it's an expression of certain principles of action, it's an effect of something. But until now, we've defined the cycle as a shadow of these processes in particular, the action of the Sun; actions on the Earth, within the Earth, the ocean systems, what have you, action of life.

Well, what happens when we see evidence for changes, for variations which we can't attribute to any of these previously known principles? What happens when we see variations which we can't account for in our current hypothesized understanding of the causes governing the system?

This is really what we've been talking about for the past month on these shows, and on larouchepac.com. We're presenting you with these indications, this ticket, this wonderful deviation, this indication that something else is going on, which we can't account for in our current understanding, indications of another factor at place, which isn't currently in our hypothesized framework, which we used to define our understanding of the cause of this shadow we call the water cycle.

These are things we've discussed: You have our current understanding of how our Solar System moves through our galaxy, through the galactic system. By the old framework, that shouldn't matter to the water cycle, that shouldn't matter to climate, that shouldn't matter to how water behaves on Earth. But we see records that there's a relationship there. We see variations, deviations in the climate records, which don't correspond to anything we can define in the prior system, the prior framework of the limitations of the principles at play.

But we do see that it corresponds to this galactic relationship. We see indications, variations showing that as the Sun changes its strength, as the Sun gets weaker, as the Sun rises and falls in its amount of activity, and lowers its shielding of the Solar System from the influence of the galaxy around us, as the Sun lets in more galactic effect, so to speak. Again, we see deviations, variations in how the water behaves, in how the water cycle operate—where you have droughts, where you have excess water; deviations, variations which don't correspond to anything in the previous system but are directly related to how the activity of the Sun interacts with this larger galactic effect.

And we see these on time-scales of thousands of years; we see these in time-scales of hundreds of years, we see these on time-scales of tens of years. We even see indications of short time-scales of days, when the Sun will release large outbursts of plasma, of solar activity, these explosive events just above the surface of the Sun, that will release large structures of plasma, coronal mass ejections. When these things pass by the Earth, they can temporarily increase the shielding around the Earth, decreasing the amount of influence from the galactic system, and we see deviations, we see variations, in how water is behaving in the atmosphere, associated with the reduction of this galactic effect, this galactic input.

So these are things we've discussed, we've presented, we've written about, but they're all indications of something which exists outside of the current framework. And until recently, most people have been operating under this earlier assumption, that the water cycle is defined by activity in the Solar System: What the Sun does, what the Earth's doing; maybe you have a role for plant life, various phenomena on the Earth affect it, but that's it. Influences beyond the Solar System have been excluded under that framework; galactic influences are believed to have no role under that framework.

But now, with the evidence we're presenting here, we're clearly seeing otherwise. We're seeing these deviations, effects which we can't attribute to the prior framework, and which directly point us to this galactic system. And this is not work that I'm doing—this is work that's been done by a relative handful of scientists, who have the guts and the strength to pursue these frontier questions, who've been showing for the recent years, that you do have these effects, you do have these deviations, it does point you to these larger cosmic processes.

And what they provided us here, is this whole framework that we're pulling together that we can present to you, which tells us we can't ignore these deviations. We see that the shadow which is the water cycle, the effect of these forces as play, which we call the water cycle, is not cast solely by activity from within the Solar System. You have the casting of the effect of activity from the galaxy as well.

The Galaxy: The 'New Frontier'

So we have to understand the water cycle from this higher perspective, we have to include the role of the galaxy. We have to think on the level of the galactic system when we think about things as we thought as simple as how the water cycle behaves. We have to recognize that this cast shadow which we depend upon, which we call the water cycle, is an expression of galactic processes, as well.

Just to be a little more specific: This changes, in particular, especially how we understand how water behaves in the atmosphere. The Sun is constantly pumping water from the ocean into the atmosphere through evaporation, filling the atmosphere with water vapor. This is now giving us new insights into how that water behaves when it's in the atmospheric system. And most importantly, for the situation now, today, this gives us new insights into how we can begin to influence and control, what we should really call the cosmic environment of the atmosphere; how we can begin to influence and control, ourselves, the conditions of the atmosphere which we otherwise attribute to the activity of the galactic system.

And again, this is something we've discussed over the past month: We have these so-called ionization systems, these systems that have been developed and successfully utilized to affect and modulate these what I would call "cosmic" conditions, or the "cosmic environment," of the atmosphere, to influence how the water behaves up there. We've discussed the success of these systems. We've shown that we can increase precipitation; we've shown that we can bring in new flows of atmospheric moisture, over the land, bring it from above the oceans, above the land. We've shown that we can begin to tap into this vast potential of the atmo-

NASA

To solve the water crisis, not only in California and the U.S. West, but throughout the world, we have to look to the galactic system, as a start. This NASA photo shows the American continent surrounded by abundant water.

spheric water system.

But the way we're doing so, is again, by controlling the conditions of the atmosphere, which are created by, and associated with, the effect of this galactic system, that we're affecting and influencing the cosmic environment of our atmosphere.

So I would say, look at this the way Kepler would. We've been discussing some of the effects here, some of the particulars, but how would Kepler see this? As Megan stated very well in the introduction, Kepler demonstrated, mankind is not an animal: Mankind is not bound by his sense-perceptual or biological experience, the way every animal species that we know of is. Mankind is gifted with a unique capability of the human mind, something which exists outside of and beyond the senses. And it's the ability to generate creative actions by the human mind, unique to the human mind itself, which is what enables mankind to make these changes, to fundamentally change how we relate to the universe.

If you mention the Solar System, foolish people think of the Solar System as some array of objects individually floating around in some big void of space; that's their conception of the Solar System. What did Kepler show us? He said, that's a shadow, those are effects. They're the result of a cause. And it's mankind that can uniquely understand that cause, and understand that cause in a way that we can act in that domain, of cause; act in the domain of that which generates the effects, generates the shadows.

It's not about the size of the space or the scale of the time, the way people normally think of these terms. It's a different conception: It's about, where does the generative principle exist? What is it, how can we understand it? And how can mankind generate his own similar effects, and utilize them, and express himself as that type of force in the universe? How can mankind cast his own shadows of creative action, not just react to other shadows?

So I think this is the type of conception that Kepler gives us that we absolutely need today, because, you know, he didn't solve everything—and I don't think he would have wanted to solve everything. I think he would have enjoyed the idea of new challenges, looking to the galaxy, looking to the supergalactic structure that we're encompassed by.

Today, we have to look to this next frontier; we have to look to the galactic system, as a start. Again, not as a collection of objects, a collection of different things, but we have to make an effort to understand what are the principles generating this system, this process, these effects, in the unique way we see it expressed. And how can we not just try to define it in some academic sense, but how can we look to act in that domain? How can we think of mankind as moving toward the potentials of casting shadows of creative action, associated with what we might call a galactic principle? That's the level that mankind is now looking at, the level that mankind can go to.

So if we want water, if we want water for California, if we want to solve the water crisis in California and other regions, other states, other parts of the world, we have to be human. We have to be like Kepler.

'Silk Road Lady' Intensifies Campaign To Make U.S. and Europe Join the BRICS

May 4—In a webcast and three major conferences in European cities during the last week in April, Schiller Institute founder Helga Zepp-LaRouche spoke along with leading representatives of the BRICS nations, insisting the United States and Europe must join the BRICS in a new system for war-avoidance and credit for infrastructure.

Zepp-LaRouche welcomed the recent mass decisions by nearly all European nations to join the China-initiated Asian Infrastructure Investment Bank (AIIB), defying the Obama Administration in doing so. They demonstrate the potential to break Europe out of the grip of economic stagnation, deadly austerity policies, and NATO's war confrontation with Russia.

"I think that there is a fundamental shift," she reported, "because people realize that Europe, without Russia and China, as part of Eurasia, is simply not going to survive, and people really see that the future is in these countries."

But the realization demands that European nations reject the war policy, create new credit institutions and join China and the BRICS in building "land-bridge" development corridors across Eurasia, linking East Asia and Europe by land and sea and developing the landlocked nations between them.

Zepp-LaRouche became known in China as "the Silk Road Lady" for her 30-year campaign for this. She told an audience including many diplomats in Copenhagen Apr. 27, that she "jumped that

high" for joy when President Xi Jinping announced it, as China's "Economic Belt and Road" infrastructure investment policy in October 2013.

Since that time she has waged an intensifying campaign in Europe for the new system of mutual economic and scientific development of nations which this offers, as the alternative to war and potential thermonuclear war confrontation.

"There is an increase in curiosity, because the effort to force Europe to impose sanctions against Russia, has led to a tremendous backfire in Germany, in France, in Italy, and other countries, in Austria," Zepp-LaRouche said. "Because people realize that these sanctions hurt themselves, their industries, much more than even Russia, because Russia is turning to Asia.

"So people also, step by step, perceive that China

Cultural Business Dialogue

The Cultural-Business Dialogue in Baden-Baden, Germany, one of a number of major presentations on the "new system" of the BRICS by Helga Zepp-LaRouche (at podium) in recent weeks.

has done an economic miracle, which is really almost as spectacular, if not more, than the German economic miracle in the post-War period. And also India is taking off, and these perspectives have become extremely active, especially the idea that there will be, in the next immediate period, an eight trillion euro investment potential in the BRICS countries. And despite the block by the media, it is penetrating, and it creates an enormous optimism."

'Hint of Spring'

The Twentieth Century was disastrous for Europe. With her Twenty-first Century Silk Road/Eurasian Land-Bridge campaign, Zepp-LaRouche is reigniting Europe's "American" economic development impetus of the late Nineteenth Century.

Then, the world-changing success of Alexander Hamilton's 'American System' in the United States, led European leaders like Bismarck and Russia's Count Witte to apply its principles in rail-building, port development, creation of new manufacturing industries, etc., and radiated it into Japan and Korea as well.

Now after a century of the "British System" of monetarism, free trade, depressions, wars, and population reduction, the China-led BRICS new development paradigm offers a new 'Hamiltonian' chance.

"I think it reflects itself in a growing recognition that we have been the spark and the idea-givers for many of these things," Zepp-LaRouche said, "so that the event in Baden-Baden was very important. People appreciated my several interventions very much, and there is a deep recognition in Russia about Lyn's economic policies, which goes way back. And in Copenhagen, we had eight ambassadors at the event, and eight more embassies, and many thinktanks and industrialists, and Schiller members. So it was an extremely optimistic event, and people really had hint of spring, which lies in all of these ideas.

The 'Good News'

Following her Apr. 21 European webcast and her speech Apr. 24 to the Cultural-Business Dialogue in Baden-Baden, Germany, (http://www.larouchepub.com/pr/2015/150428_helga_baden_baden.html) Zepp-LaRouche spoke together with a number of Chinese representatives including its ambassador, to a large seminar at the Copenhagen Business Confucius Institute Apr. 27; and then to a major *EIR* seminar in Frankfurt Apr. 28.

The proceedings in Frankfurt show the impact her campaign is having. As she noted, "We had four developing countries represented through large trade organizations, or consulates, and they all expressed very determined goals as to when they want to be either a fully industrialized country, or when they want to be at least medium-developed; but there is no longer the idea that they can be prevented from their development. A very optimistic spirit was also visible there."

The speakers representing those four nations were Prof. Shi Ze, Senior Research Fellow at the China Institute of International Studies; former Greek ambassador and diplomat Leonidas Chrysanthopoulos; Malaysian Investment Development Agency director S. Sundara Raja; and the Ethiopian Consul-General in Frankfurt. Other diplomats were in the audience of 75 at the seminar.

All the speakers agreed that they no longer listen to the dubious and destructive advice of the IMF experts, monetarist bankers and "geopoliticians," but focus on policies that serve the development of their nations' real economy and the well-being of their citizens. They view the grouping of BRICS-allied nations as a great growth and development potential that will be tapped.

Zepp-LaRouche opened the Frankfurt seminar by offering the "good news" that the BRICS development and the LaRouche movement are providing an alternative to the collapsing Wall Street-London dominated system—which even the IMF now predicts, is facing yet another crash. With bank and government credit dried up in the West, the many new international development banks being created by the BRICS countries are initiating the huge investments for "great projects" of infrastructure which are urgently needed, she said.

Zepp-LaRouche described how her husband, *EIR* Founding Editor Lyndon LaRouche, had proposed such an International Development Bank and its necessary great projects 40 years ago; and that those projects and development corridors would have been built, had banks done their job of serving the real economy with credit. China now repeatedly invites Europe—and the United States—to join and help capitalize the development banks the BRICS are creating.

The "Silk Road Lady" emphasized that Chinese political thought includes the Confucian principles of collaboration and harmony of nations, underlying both China's massive development strides, and its offers of collaboration in a new credit system to the West.

In Germany's business and financial capital of Frankfurt, Zepp-LaRouche addressed an April 28 seminar with representatives of China, Greece, Malaysia, and Ethiopia.

EIRNS/Christopher Lewis

Prof. Shi Ze located the "New Silk Road" policy of China within the fact—of crucial importance for the economic future now—that after the 2008 crash of the trans-Atlantic banks, China dramatically *increased* its involvement (credit and investment), becoming a global economic driver, while some other regions' contributions collapsed.

The Chinese expert presented a "nested" series of spheres of this credit and development: first, the drive to break down the once-vast differences in living standards between eastern China and its rural, partially desert West; second, the economic development of the landlocked Central Asian republics through the "New Silk Road"; third, the development through the AIIB of all of South Asia from ASEAN to the Middle East, and even Southeast Europe—"giving the America economy new opportunities and markets." He explained that for China itself, the New Silk Road represents a new responsibility in world politics, for the creation of a new international community around a common principle of mutual economic and scientific progress.

Whoever doesn't understand the New Silk Road in this way, said Prof. Shi, does not understand China.

Greece Offers Its Potential

Greek ambassador Leonidas Chrysanthopoulos presented the seminar with the most sobering possible picture of the economic desolation which must be overcome in Europe—the damage which the EU has done to the Greek economy and Greek people since 2002, causing the "downgrading of human rights of Greeks" as documented by human rights organizations. He stressed that every agency from the IMF to the UN to the ECB, and every government in Europe including the Greek government, allowed economic austerity to remove human rights guaranteed under every European treaty and convention. "What went wrong with the EU?" Chrysanthopoulos asked. "Why is it destroying its member-states and peoples?"

"An answer to this may be the BRICS initiative," he said. "This is an initiative of Brazil, Russia, India, China and South Africa to pursue a policy of economic development for the benefit of humanity. To that end they have created a Development Bank to invest billions in necessary development projects. China recently initiated the Asian Infrastructure Investment Bank (AIIB), joined by over 20 Asian nations as founding members, and has set up a Silk Road Development Fund. China has also proposed within BRICS the creation of a Free Trade Area of Asia and the Pacific (FTAAP).The incorporation of the Shanghai Cooperation Organization into the BRICS initiative could create a formidable power, which if it remains out of the control of the bankers and big companies' lobbyists, could lead to a point that humanity indeed has a chance to reach global peace and end poverty through common human economic development."

Noting the "desperate need for the cooperation of the U.S.A. and ... Europe with the BRICS countries and their initiatives," the ambassador added: "Because of Greece's special relationships with China and Russia, Athens can play an important role within the BRICS initiative."

Along the same lines, the head of the Malaysian Investment Development Agency's head, Siva Sundara Raja, explained how Malaysia had learned from recent experience to ignore the instructions of the IMF and the London/Wall Street banking "consensus."

That painful experience was the 1997-98 so-called "Asian financial crisis," in which Malaysia's previous 40 years' manufaturing and technology development took a sharp backwards blow, because its financial policies had come from the IMF and western banking "experts." Rejecting this "consensus" under Prime Minister Dr. Mahathir Mohammad, Malaysia imposed capital and currency controls and stopped offshore speculation in its currency. Only then could it resume is economic growth dynamic.

Not accidentally, this policy of capital and currency controls—*and Glass-Steagall separation of its banks*— has been the policy of China throughout its last 25 years' astonishing economic, scientific, and technological growth.

Effect of Joining the BRICS

The final and very important seminar contribution was made by Ethiopia's consul-general in Frankfurt, Mehreteab Mulugeta Haile. Since its 1991 hunger crisis, he explained, Ethiopia has concentrated on strengthening nationally important economic branches—a "Hamiltonian" policy—and has now

again reached food self-sufficiency. The country's economic growth rates have rivalled those of China, recently at the level of 11% with plans to increase this further.

Mulugeta Haile said that his country sees collaboration with the BRICS as crucial to its present and future growth. Russian, Indian, and Brazilian credits are financing railroad projects, and China's investment credits for Africa are available to fund new Ethiopian infrastructure projects. The African Union, he said, plans a paradigm shift for the next 50 years, based on this assistance in economic development.

The crucial question of China's overall Africa policy—outside the "Silk Road" belts, but included in China's "vision and action plan" for Eurasian development—was raised from the seminar audience. Dr. Shi—who had also spoken together with Helga Zepp-LaRouche at the Baden-Baden conference—said that although in Europe's media, China's Africa policy is called "imperialist," in Africa it is seen as partnership for the development of agriculture, modern transport, communications, education and healthcare.

The Frankfurt audience was fully engaged for three and one-half hours in the strategy of reversing Europe's self-destructive recent policy; and at the conclusion, were anxious to know from Zepp-LaRouche and her colleagues, what the next public steps would be.

On the U.S.: 'You Really Have to Fight for It'

May 2—In the midst of her European mobilization, Helga Zepp-LaRouche was asked her view, from Europe, of the "Manhattan Project," the campaign of LaRouche PAC and the Schiller Institute to restore "Alexander Hamilton's New York" as the center of the fight to restore Hamilton's credit and general welfare principles. She has keynoted three major events in New York in the past year.

Her answer was blunt:

I think it would be extremely important for our readers to really reckon with the fact that the image of the United States around the world is at a historic low. And that is obviously the result of a long, long time of Bush senior, a short interruption with the Clinton years, and then two Bush administrations, and now six years of Obama. The image people have about the United States is that the United States has conducted one war after the other, based on lies—Iraq, Afghanistan, Libya, Syria. It has resulted in the complete hellhole destruction of these countries, as a result of which Europe is now being flooded with thousands and thousands of refugees from Iraq, from Syria, from Africa. In a certain sense, people really do not see any positive thing about the United States at all.

Secondly, there is right now a huge scandal, which is rocking the transAtlantic relations even more than the Snowden affair, because it came out that the BND collaborated with the NSA in spying on political leaders in France, Austria, Brussels, and this has led to a really big upheaval.... [People] say this is an unbelievable mess, as disgrace, and, to say it diplomatically, an unbelievable stupidity. Obviously, we have to have a full investigation. Was the German BND pressured? Were they threatened? The fact that there was economic espionage against Airbus— we are not the enemy! So, it's really—officials of the United States are so arrogant by now, that they think that they can continue to do this forever, and it will have no effect.

But I see clear cracks, growing cracks, in the alliance, and if you keep doing things which feed the mistrust, this will not last forever.... Because if this thing is continued, and leads to global war; if there's a thermonuclear destruction, then it's a moot question because nobody will ask that question afterwards. But if it's anything less than that, Americans will have to ask themselves: Why did they allow this to go on for so long, with such terrible consequences around the world?

So, therefore, people should really uphold this Manhattan project, because this *is* the effort to regain the soul of America, to turn the United States back into a republic, and give it back its beautiful identity which was meant to be. But people really have to fight now, because it's not there. It's a potential, but people really have to fight.